I0821903

DONALD **TRUMP**

45th US President

BY JAMES STUART

CONTENT CONSULTANT
RACHEL BLUM, PhD
DEPARTMENT OF POLITICAL SCIENCE
UNIVERSITY OF OKLAHOMA

Essential Library

An Imprint of Abdo Publishing | abdobooks.com

abdobooks.com

Published by Abdo Publishing, a division of ABDO, PO Box 398166, Minneapolis, Minnesota 55439.

Printed in the United States of America, North Mankato, Minnesota.
102020
012021

Cover Photo: Evan Vucci/AP Images
Interior Photos: Alex Brandon/AP Images, 4; J. Scott Applewhite/AP Images, 7; Evan Vucci/AP Images, 10, 67, 76; Seth Poppel/Yearbook Library, 12, 18; Drew Angerer/Getty Images News/Getty Images, 16; Dennis Caruso/New York Daily News Archive/Getty, 22; AP Images, 27; Leif Skoogfors/Corbis Historical/Getty Images, 32; Marty Lederhandler/AP Images, 37, 50; Time & Life Pictures/The LIFE Picture Collection/Getty Images, 38; Mario Suriani/AP Images, 41; Wilbur Funches/AP Images, 42; Jon McNally/Hulton Archive/Getty Images, 46; NBC/Photofest, 53; Christopher Gregory/Getty Images News/Getty Images, 58; Patrick Semansky/AP Images, 63, 86; Anthony Behar/Sipa USA/AP Images, 68; Olivier Douliery/Abaca/Sipa USA/AP Images, 72; Kyodo/AP Images, 78; Yuri Gripas/Abaca/Sipa USA/AP Images, 93; Chris Kleponis/Polaris/picture-alliance/dpa/AP Images, 95

Editor: Arnold Ringstad
Series Designer: Becky Daum

Library of Congress Control Number: 2020940268

Publisher's Cataloging-in-Publication Data

Names: Stuart, James, author.
Title: Donald Trump: 45th US President / by James Stuart
Other title: 45th US President
Description: Minneapolis, Minnesota : Abdo Publishing, 2021 | Series: Essential lives | Includes online resources and index
Identifiers: ISBN 9781532194115 (lib. bdg.) | ISBN 9781098213473 (ebook)
Subjects: LCSH: Trump, Donald, 1946---Juvenile literature. | Legislators--United States--Biography--Juvenile literature. | Presidents--United States--Biography--Juvenile literature.
Classification: DDC 973.933--dc23

CONTENTS

CHAPTER 1
A NEW KIND OF PRESIDENT 4

CHAPTER 2
GROWING UP TRUMP 12

CHAPTER 3
BUILDING NEW YORK 22

CHAPTER 4
GAMBLING ON THE FUTURE 32

CHAPTER 5
BUILDING THE BRAND 42

CHAPTER 6
BRANCHING OUT 50

CHAPTER 7
MAKE AMERICA GREAT AGAIN 58

CHAPTER 8
PRESIDENT TRUMP 68

CHAPTER 9
A TUMULTUOUS FINAL YEAR 82

Timeline 96
Essential Facts 100
Glossary 102
Additional Resources 104
Source Notes 106
Index 110
About the Author 112
About the Consultant 112

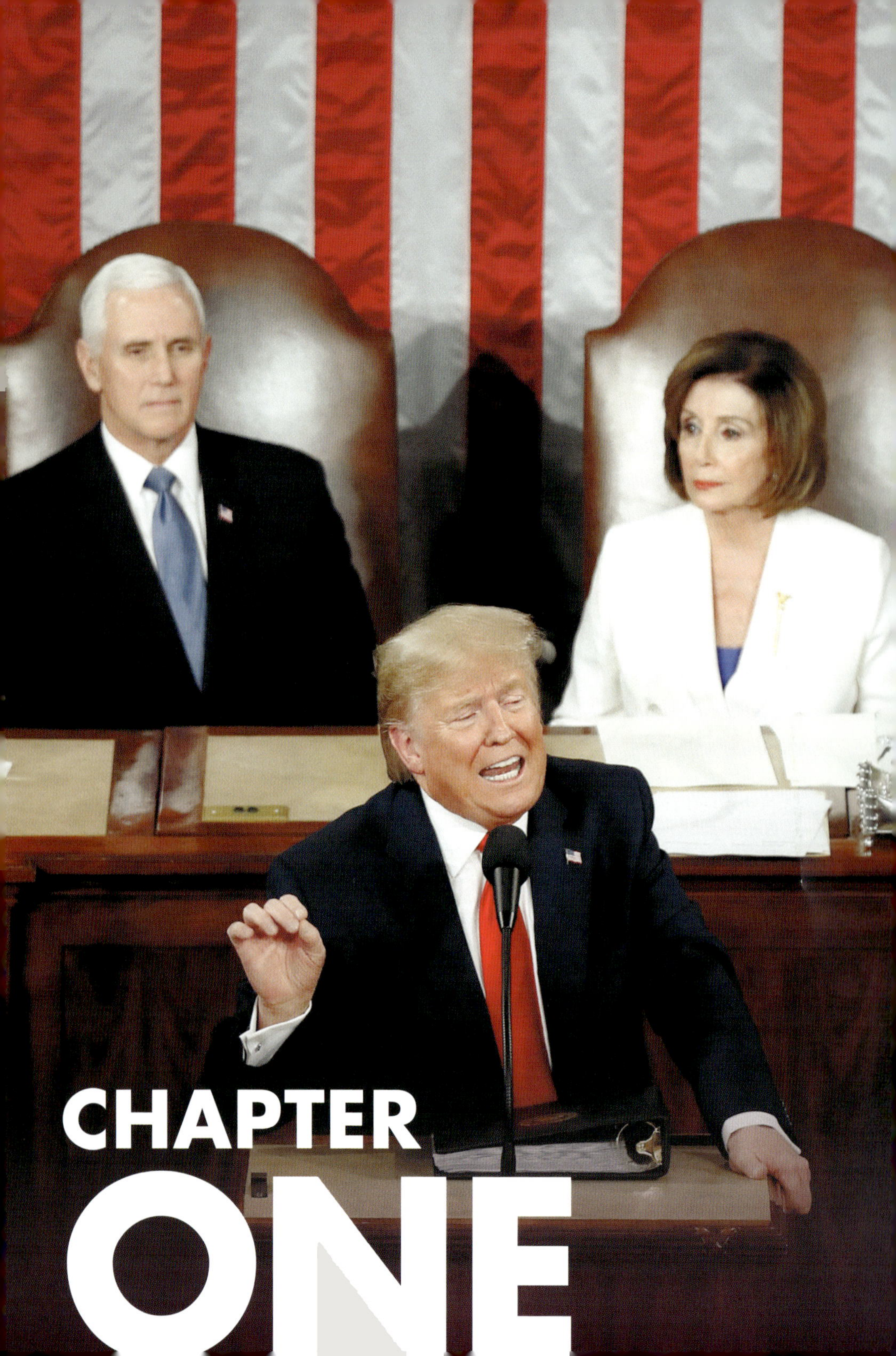

CHAPTER ONE

A NEW KIND OF PRESIDENT

The chamber of the US House of Representatives echoed with applause as President Donald Trump entered the room to deliver his third State of the Union address. It was February 4, 2020. As he approached the podium, the chamber was filled with tension. Republicans in the room chanted "four more years" in reference to Trump's bid for reelection. Democrats sat silently. Republicans and Democrats were fiercely divided over Trump's policies. Following tradition, the speaker of the House, Democrat Nancy Pelosi, reached out to shake Trump's hand when he arrived at the front of the room. He ignored her.

Pelosi returned the snub. Typically, the speaker of the House introduces the president by saying she or he has the "high privilege and distinct honor of presenting to you the president of the United States." Pelosi left

Entering the fourth year of his presidency, Donald Trump used his State of the Union address to highlight his administration's record on national security and the economy.

out the ceremonial language, instead simply saying, "the president of the United States."[1]

Trump's speech laid out what he described as the "incredible results" of the "great American comeback."[2] He said his administration had created more than seven million new jobs, reduced unemployment, increased wages, cracked down on unfair trade practices, improved national security, and led the fight against terrorism globally. "I am thrilled to report to you tonight that our economy is the best it has ever been. . . . Our borders are secure. Our families are flourishing. Our values are renewed. Our pride is restored," Trump boasted.[3] He did not mention his recent impeachment, in which the House accused him of abuse of power and obstruction of Congress. The Senate was soon due to vote on whether to remove him from office.

The speech prompted standing ovations on several occasions, but many Democrats didn't stand or clap. It was their way of protesting Trump's policies. Some Democratic members of Congress chose not to attend the event, and others walked out of the chamber during the address. When Trump was finished, Pelosi tore up a printed copy of the speech. Her prominent position

The sharply differing reactions to Trump's 2020 State of the Union address highlighted the stark political divisions in the country.

directly behind Trump made it a highly visible gesture for television cameras and people in the room. These acts of protest illustrated the deep political tension in the United States throughout Trump's presidency.

An Outsider

Trump hadn't followed the traditional political career path of being elected to offices of increasing importance and responsibility on the way to becoming president. He was a businessperson. When he announced his bid for the presidency in 2015, he was quick to separate himself from mainstream politicians. He described them in his announcement speech as "morally corrupt" and "controlled fully by the lobbyists."[4] Trump didn't have political experience, making him an outsider in political circles. But he suggested that his business experience made him uniquely qualified to make the big changes he felt Americans were demanding. He referred to the United States as a "brand" which he would make "great again."[5]

Trump's lack of political experience made him an unlikely candidate for president, but many Americans were frustrated with the government and traditional politicians. In 2015, only 19 percent of

FROM BUSINESS TO THE PRESIDENCY

Donald Trump often spoke of his business experience during his campaign. He was not the first business leader to run for the office of president. Several former presidents ran businesses before holding the nation's highest office. President George W. Bush and his father, President George H. W. Bush, were both in the oil business. The younger Bush also co-owned baseball's Texas Rangers. Harry S. Truman owned a men's clothing company. Warren Harding operated a newspaper. Herbert Hoover ran a mining company, and Calvin Coolidge was vice president of a bank in western Massachusetts.

Americans said they trusted the government most or all of the time.[6] Given this context, it was not surprising that antiestablishment candidates became contenders in the presidential race. In the decades leading up to the 2016 election, many people on either the conservative or liberal side of the political spectrum felt they had little common ground with those on the other. Trump appealed to a Republican electorate that wanted to see a major change in US leadership.

Many of Trump's campaign proposals were controversial. In December 2015 he called for a ban on Muslims entering the United States as a way to counter terrorism, and he proposed to eliminate the US Department of Education to cut spending. He promised to build a wall along the US–Mexico border to stop undocumented immigration, and he declared that Mexico would pay for it. The media, many Republicans, and Democrats criticized Trump's plans. They accused the policies of being contradictory, unconstitutional, and racist. Trump supporters disagreed. Businessperson Essie Dube summed up the feelings of many Trump supporters: "Donald Trump may be a little rough around the edges . . . but he says it like it is. He says things

Trump developed and maintained a passionate base of support during his campaign and his presidency.

that other Americans are afraid to say but they feel in their heart."[7]

From his upbringing in the business world to his unusual success on the political scene, Donald Trump has forged an unconventional life and career. For both supporters and critics, he became the center of attention in American public life. In the course of Trump's one-term presidency, he put his distinct mark on American history.

TRUMP SUPPORTERS

Trump does not fit the mold of most politicians who have served in the US government. He routinely makes controversial comments, stretches the truth, and brags about his wealth and successes. Though he differs from candidates who came before him, he found a base of support in the 2016 election and throughout his presidency.

Political experts and members of the media studied Trump's appeal. They believed some people liked that Trump, unlike most presidential candidates, offered to fund his own campaign instead of relying on donors. Other supporters appreciated that he was not a career politician, so he could bring new ideas to government. He also spoke bluntly, which people preferred to the slick, polished comments typical of politicians. The bulk of Trump's support came from white, working-class voters without college degrees. This group makes up more than 40 percent of the nation's voters.[8]

CHAPTER TWO

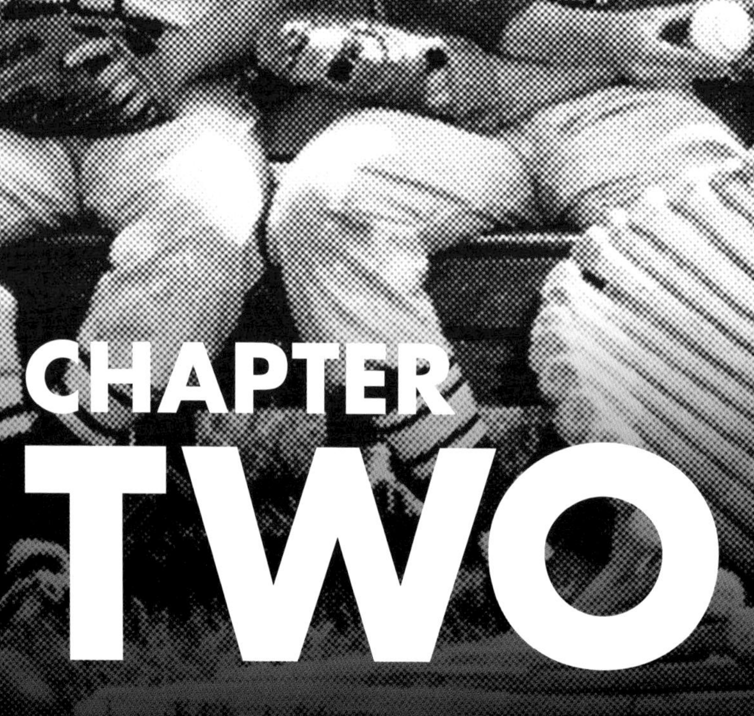

GROWING UP TRUMP

Donald John Trump was born on June 14, 1946, to parents Mary Anne and Fred Trump. He had two older sisters, Maryanne and Elizabeth. Donald also had an older brother, Fred Jr., and a younger brother, Robert.

The Trump family lived in the upper-middle-class neighborhood of Jamaica Estates in Queens, New York City. When Donald was born, the Trumps lived on Wareham Place in a modest home. But Fred was hard at work on a much larger home on the large lot behind their house. Eventually, it would have 23 rooms and nine bathrooms.[1] The building project was not a new endeavor for Fred. He had been constructing affordable, middle-class apartment complexes and homes in Queens and Brooklyn since the late 1920s.

Trump, *center*, played many sports while in high school.

Fred Trump

Fred was a shrewd businessperson and a hands-on builder. He was the son of German immigrants who were successful entrepreneurs. His father had started a small real estate business when he moved to Queens in 1908. When Fred's father died in 1918, Fred aimed to run the family business. He took construction classes at the local YMCA while finishing high school. After graduating in 1923, he took over the business.

Fred spent the next few years obtaining private loans to fund modest family homes. When the Great Depression (1929–1939) reduced demand for homes, Fred opened a grocery store in Queens. He got back into the real estate business in the 1930s, but this time, he did not do it alone. Instead, Fred built relationships with local politicians and bankers. They helped him get the best terms for his construction projects.

BE A KILLER

Fred Trump was known by his family, friends, and colleagues to be driven, tough, and demanding. He took his business seriously, and he always dressed in a suit and cuff links, even on weekends. He also took his family's success seriously. Fred pushed Donald to be a "killer," leading by example in his dealings with local politicians and pushing for real estate tax breaks.[2] Donald took these skills with him when he expanded the Trump real estate business into Manhattan.

The projects took advantage of new government programs that promoted homeownership, designed to bolster the country's struggling economy.

Young Donald

By the time Donald was born in 1946, Fred was a prominent builder in Queens and Brooklyn. He was also a tireless, driven businessperson. During Donald's childhood, Fred worked long hours. He spent 12 to 14 hours every workday visiting building sites and networking with politicians and government officials. Frequently, Donald and his siblings accompanied Fred on weekend trips to jobsites, picking up stray nails as their father saved money by performing maintenance himself.

Fred was a taskmaster at home too. Donald and his siblings had strict curfews and were not allowed to eat between meals. Fred encouraged his children to be mindful of costs at home, just as he was at his jobsites. Donald and his siblings had summer jobs, collected bottles to cash in on the deposit, and were instructed to clean their plates at meals. He also told his children to learn how positive thinking can create success, an idea

Trump's childhood home on Wareham Place in Queens, New York City

outlined in the popular 1952 book *The Power of Positive Thinking* by minister and author Norman Vincent Peale.

When Donald was five, Fred and Mary Anne enrolled him in a local private school, Kew-Forest School. He was a sociable, outgoing child who got into mischief. At Kew-Forest, he met his childhood best friend, Peter Brant. The two of them soon earned reputations as pranksters, ignoring their studies to shoot spitballs and throw stink bombs. A classmate remembers Donald got in trouble so often that detentions at Kew-Forest became known as DTs, or "Donny Trumps." By the time Donald was 13, the school—and Fred—were fed up with Donald paying more attention to pranks than schoolwork. For eighth grade, Donald would attend the New York Military Academy (NYMA), 55 miles (89 km) from his home.[3]

Thriving with Structure and Competition

The NYMA had a reputation for turning unruly young men into disciplined, successful students. In his five years at the school, that is exactly what happened to Donald. He thrived in the structured environment, where he and his classmates lived in barracks and were awakened by a bugle each morning. In class, in the barracks, and on the sports field, competitiveness and aggression were highly valued. Donald excelled at athletics. As an older student, he was ruthless when it was his job to inspect the barracks.

Summer vacation from the NYMA was not idle time for Donald. Summers were devoted to learning the basics of the family real estate business. He eagerly helped his father on jobsites around Queens and Brooklyn. He worked at one of his father's apartment complexes. He was responsible for making sure the

The strict, competitive atmosphere at the New York Military Academy helped shape Trump's character.

building and its units were well maintained. He also drove his dad to and from his daily meetings.

Donald often accompanied his father to Cincinnati, Ohio, where Fred had purchased a run-down apartment complex called Swifton Village. These visits were an education in themselves. Donald observed Fred's drive and tough style with the crews on the jobsite. Fred allowed Donald to negotiate maintenance contracts with potential vendors and collect rent from tenants. He emphasized professionalism and the value of hands-on management of jobsites.

COLLECTING RENT

During his time at Swifton, Trump collected rent from tenants. The area was rough. "One of the first tricks I learned was that you never stand in front of someone's door when you knock," recalled Trump. "Instead you stand by the wall and reach over to knock."[4] One of the men training Trump explained why he should do it this way. "If you stand to the side, the only thing exposed to danger is your hand. . . . In this business, if you knock on the wrong apartment at the wrong time, you're liable to get shot."[5]

Off to College

After graduating from the NYMA, Trump enrolled at Fordham University in the Bronx. Donald's studies at Fordham were not going as well as his work with Fred. He had a difficult time fitting in at the school. Donald did not smoke or drink, as many of his peers did, and his extravagant wealth set him apart from his fellow students. In 1966, after two years at Fordham, he transferred to the Wharton School of Business at the University of Pennsylvania.

The Wharton School had a small but strong real estate department—one of only a few such departments in the nation at the time. Trump competed fiercely with his classmates, most of whom were from real estate

THE VIETNAM WAR DRAFT

In June 1964, Trump turned 18. Like all other 18-year-old American men, the law required him to register with the Selective Service System. This government agency keeps track of men eligible for military service. When Trump registered, the United States was fighting in the Vietnam War (1954–1975). A draft looked likely.

Trump received four deferments while in college, one for each year he was a student. It meant he would not have to serve in the military. When Trump graduated in 1968, his deferments ended. The government was poised to call a draft. The fall after graduation, Trump received a medical deferment for bone spurs in his heel. It kept him out of the draft. For men of Trump's generation, seeking deferments was common. Approximately 60 percent of men worked to get some kind of deferment during the Vietnam War.[6]

The circumstances around Trump's medical deferment are unclear. Trump said that a doctor wrote him a letter about the bone spurs and that Trump presented that letter to draft officials. In later interviews, Trump was unable to recall the name of the doctor and declined to provide documentation. In 2018, the daughters of a New York podiatrist told the *New York Times* that their father had written the letter as a favor to Fred Trump, but they had no definitive evidence of such an arrangement. Critics claim Donald got a fake diagnosis to avoid being drafted and did not do his patriotic duty. "I think I've made a lot of sacrifices," he said in response to those who said he had not sacrificed anything for the country. "I work very, very hard. I've created thousands and thousands of jobs . . . built great structures. I've had tremendous success. I think I've done a lot."[7]

families similar to the Trumps. Donald graduated from the Wharton School on May 20, 1968. He walked off the graduation stage and onto the stage of commercial real estate.

Starting Out at Swifton

Donald's first job after college was managing Swifton Village, the run-down 1,200-unit apartment complex Fred had purchased in 1964. Fred's company renovated the property, and two years later the apartment complex was full. Now, it was his son's turn to manage the property.

Donald moved to Cincinnati to manage Swifton Village. He spent his first summer after college supervising projects on the property. Employees remember Trump rolling up his sleeves and helping with landscaping and other projects. In his 1987 book, *The Art of the Deal*, he describes the turnaround of Swifton Village as his first big deal. But Trump had his sights set on something much bigger. He dreamed of developing real estate in Manhattan.

CHAPTER THREE

BUILDING NEW YORK

After a summer focusing on Swifton Village, Trump shifted his attention to helping his father with the New York properties. His main role was collecting rent from tenants of Trump Management Corporation properties. Trump describes the experience of going door-to-door to collect rent as unpleasant and, at times, violent.

In 1973, Trump became the president of Trump Management Corporation. The company owned more than 14,000 apartments in Queens, Brooklyn, and Staten Island, New York City.[1]

The Trump Philosophy

Though he had an Ivy League business degree, Trump's business philosophy came from his father. The hard-driving builder worked tirelessly to develop his real estate business. His specialty was renovating

Trump learned many of the skills he needed in real estate from his father, Fred.

run-down properties. He made them appeal to working-class families who hoped to move up to the middle class. Always a frugal man, he improved a property's quality without adding frivolous extras. Fred demanded work be done precisely and cost effectively.

Fred looked for ways to bring the costs of properties down. Early on, he realized the best way to reduce costs was to negotiate tax breaks for his projects. It was not an easy task. To do it, he spent time getting to know New York's most powerful politicians. He funded campaigns for governor and Congress. He sat on powerful boards, such as the one for the Brooklyn Borough Gas Company. All of this earned Fred influence with local politicians. In turn, they made it easier for him to make profitable deals on properties. When his son entered the family business, Donald inherited these connections.

FRUGAL FRED

When Fred Trump died in 1999, Donald Trump shared a story about his father that illustrated Fred's frugality and ingenuity. The thousands of apartments Trump Management maintained required the company to buy cleaning products in bulk. But the cost of these products added up. Trump remembers finding his father in his office, his desk covered in bottles of floor cleaner. Fred sent the bottles to a lab to discover their chemical formulas and then used the results to create his own. Instead of paying two dollars a bottle, he paid fifty cents.[2]

A Federal Lawsuit

Business was not always smooth going. On the morning of October 15, 1973, Trump received a distressing phone call. The US Department of Justice was on the line warning him it was filing a lawsuit against Trump Management for violating the Fair Housing Act of 1968.

The Fair Housing Act made it illegal for landlords to discriminate on the basis of race, color, religion, gender, or national origin. The lawsuit alleged Trump Management refused to rent apartments to African Americans. It also charged that the company had offered potential tenants different lease terms depending on the color of their skin.

In his first time quoted in the *New York Times* newspaper, Trump declared the charges "absolutely ridiculous."[3] He hired his friend and attorney Roy Cohn to represent Trump Management. Cohn countersued the US government over what he said were irresponsible and baseless charges that singled out Trump Management because it was a large, successful company.

The government and Trump Management resolved the lawsuit in a 1975 agreement. In it, Trump Management agreed to supply the New York Urban

League, a group representing disadvantaged New Yorkers, with a list of vacant apartments every week for two years. The agreement also made it clear that Trump Management was not guilty of the charges brought against it.

Making a Mark on Manhattan

By the time the lawsuit was resolved, Trump had begun making his mark on Manhattan. At the time, Manhattan's economy was struggling. Many properties were in distress, including high-profile ones such as the Chrysler Building and Grand Central Terminal. Fred had no interest in taking a gamble on these buildings. But his son saw opportunity. Trump persuaded Fred to financially support his foray into Manhattan real estate.

In 1976, Trump purchased his first Manhattan property, the bankrupt Commodore Hotel. In making the deal, Trump took a move out of his father's playbook: using tax laws to his advantage. He pressed city officials to provide huge tax breaks for the project. In exchange, his new hotel would improve a run-down part of the city. Trump's Commodore Hotel project became Manhattan's first commercial property to receive a 40-year tax abatement from the government.[4]

Trump, *left*, worked with influential figures such as New York City mayor Ed Koch, *second from left*, New York governor Hugh Carey, *pointing*, and executive Robert T. Dormer, *right*, to complete the Commodore Hotel project.

Work began on the project in 1978. Workers gutted the Commodore and renovated it into a 1,400-room hotel that appealed to wealthy guests. It opened two years later as the Grand Hyatt Hotel. For the work, Manhattan's Community Board Five gave Trump an award for the "tasteful and creative recycling of a distinguished hotel."[5] The project revitalized the neighborhood. It also gave Trump a taste of the opportunity that awaited him in the Manhattan housing market.

A Young Family

The 1970s were not all work for Trump. Over the decade, he had cultivated a reputation as a young, hotshot builder. He belonged to clubs that catered to the wealthy and drove a Cadillac with the license plate "DJT"—his initials.

In 1976, Trump met Ivana Winklmayr. Born Ivana Zelníčková in the central European nation of Czechoslovakia, Winklmayr was a skier and fashion model. She moved to New York in 1976 to continue her modeling career. She and Trump married on April 9, 1977, after dating for nine months. On December 31, the couple welcomed its first child, Donald John Trump Jr.

IVANA

Ivana Zelníčková was a competitive athlete in Czechoslovakia from a young age. When she was 12 years old, she entered her country's national training program for skiing. In her teens, she went on to enter skiing competitions across Europe. She married skier Alfred Winklmayr but divorced a few years later. She later immigrated to Canada, where she worked as a ski instructor. In the 1970s, she shifted to modeling. She traveled to New York City as part of her career; it was there that she met Trump.

Project T

Trump's next big endeavor was the Bonwit Teller building. It had housed the Bonwit Teller & Co. department store between 1930 and 1979. The building was a well-known example of art deco design, with large limestone carvings worked into the facade of the building. This is not what attracted Trump, though. He was interested in the building's prime location, surrounded by high-end shops just three blocks from Central Park.

Trump began secret negotiations to acquire the building in 1979, calling the deal Project T. He took over the building's lease and obtained the right to rename it. In negotiations, Trump argued for an exception to the city's zoning code. He wanted to build a tower that would give tenants a two-sided view: one of Central Park and another of southern Manhattan. Such a building did not fit the strict rules that required new structures to fit into the neighborhood. To win the exception, Trump offered a second design that violated the zoning rules to an outrageous degree. The planning commission accepted Trump's first plan and waived the zoning rule.

In 1980, demolition began on Project T, which became known as Trump Tower. Not all went smoothly, though. Trump had hired the contractor Kaszycki & Sons to perform the demolition. The contractor had come in with the lowest bid for the work. It soon became obvious why the bid was so low. Kaszycki & Sons hired undocumented Polish immigrants, paying them less than half what union workers would get. The Polish workers toiled 12 to 18 hours a day, seven days a week, without hard hats.[6] In 1983, the workers sued both Kaszycki & Sons and Trump. The FBI investigated to see whether the workers had been taken advantage of.

FACADE FIASCO

Since its construction in 1929, the Bonwit Teller building had become a prominent building due to its striking facade. Two large limestone panels were examples of art deco design and featured two dancing women who stood 15 feet (4.6 m) tall.[7] When the building went up for sale, art and architecture historians hoped to preserve the artwork.

When Trump started work on Trump Tower, he promised to donate the building's historic limestone facade to the Metropolitan Museum of Art. But after a few months, the artful facade had been jackhammered away. Art lovers and historians were outraged by Trump's decision. Removing the panels was much more expensive than Trump had anticipated. It would also have led to costly delays, which would have hampered his ability to secure a highly valuable tax abatement on the project. Without the abatement, the cost of the project would have increased by $25 million.[8]

The case was finally settled out of court in 1999, costing Trump $1.375 million.[9]

Work continued on Trump Tower. In July 1982, 700 people, including the governor of New York and the mayor of New York City, toasted its near completion. To celebrate, a few of the people rode a construction elevator to the top of the building for a brunch.

Soon, Trump Tower started selling apartments to wealthy buyers. Trump spared no expense, bathing the building in luxury. High-end finishes adorned the apartments, but the showstopper was Trump Tower's public lobby. Rose-colored marble covered the floor and walls, and mirrors made the space seem large. A waterfall splashed down one wall of the lobby, inviting shoppers into the building's high-end boutiques. Perched atop all this luxury was Trump's personal 53-room penthouse.[10]

CHAPTER FOUR

GAMBLING ON THE FUTURE

Trump had made an impression on the real estate world in New York. Meanwhile, he had already begun his next project, in Atlantic City, New Jersey. The city had legalized gambling in 1978, and Trump saw an opportunity to make money there.

Trump purchased the largest lot on the strip in Atlantic City. The lot was actually three separate properties and involved 30 property owners.[1] Trump was new to the casino business, but he knew if he followed the strict local rules and regulations, he stood to make a great deal of money as a casino owner. He began constructing a casino, Trump Plaza, in 1982.

Harrah's, an established casino and resort company, was looking to partner with a builder to develop its first Atlantic City property. In 1984, Harrah's and Trump opened a casino called Harrah's at Trump Plaza. The next year, the partnership collapsed.

In the 1980s, Trump believed casinos were solid investments, and he put much of his wealth into developing them.

During the partnership, Trump had been in secret negotiations with Hilton Hotel Corporation. It was a competitor of Harrah's. Trump partnered with Hilton to buy another casino, which he renamed Trump Castle. This outraged Harrah's. After some public mudslinging, Trump bought out the Harrah's stake in Trump Plaza.

IVANA TRUMP, CEO

In 1985, Trump made Ivana the CEO of Trump Castle in Atlantic City. The move ensured operations remained in the family. At the time, she had no experience running a casino. But the competitive and determined Ivana did not let lack of experience deter her. Taking a cue from her husband, Ivana actively managed Trump Castle, reviewing every detail personally and even signing the checks herself. A natural hostess, Ivana organized successful parties for the casino's high rollers. Under her leadership, Trump Castle thrived. Its revenues soon outpaced those of Trump's other Atlantic City casino, Trump Plaza.

Trump continued to invest in casinos, and in 1987 he bought a majority share in Resorts International Inc. The deal included high-risk bonds and two casinos. One casino was in the Bahamas. The other, the Taj Mahal, was still under construction in Atlantic City. Two years later, Trump sold his shares in Resorts International but kept the casinos. He had run out of money, and selling Resorts International helped him avoid bankruptcy.

Three Costly Projects

Trump's investments outside the world of gambling brought him back to Manhattan. He was interested in a 77-acre (31 ha) property known as the Yards, which ran along the Hudson River.[2] Trump had purchased the property briefly in the 1970s but was forced to sell when he did not have the funds to build on it. In 1982, Trump bought back the property and proposed a giant new project: Television City.

The plans called for several luxury skyscrapers, including a tower that would have become the tallest in the world. But the largest part of the development would be space for television studios, a shopping mall, and a giant parking lot. Television City would be the largest project undertaken in New York City since Rockefeller Center in the 1930s. Opposition from neighborhood groups and city planners put Television City on hold.

In the meantime, Trump had expanded his real estate holdings south to Palm Beach, Florida. In 1985, he purchased the $10 million mansion and beach property called Mar-a-Lago.[3] The property formerly belonged to a prominent Palm Beach family but had fallen into disrepair. In 1995, Trump turned it into a luxury resort with a high price tag for membership. He included a private area for his family.

Three years later, Trump set his sights on another property: the Plaza Hotel in Manhattan, across from Central Park and near Trump Tower. Trump paid $407.5 million for the Plaza Hotel, the highest price ever for a single hotel.[4] He also put a $125 million guarantee on the loan he took out to pay for the plaza.[5] It was a move unheard of in the real estate industry. It meant Trump would personally be responsible for $125 million if the project failed.[6]

MAR-A-LAGO

In 1995, Mar-a-Lago, Trump's personal estate in Palm Beach, Florida, opened its doors as a private club for the wealthy. Welcomed by a larger-than-life painting of Trump, members paid a one-time fee of $25,000 to join the exclusive club, a cost that has since increased.[7] Members enjoy luxurious accommodations, fine dining, a spa, a golf course, and other recreational activities.

Family Matters

The early 1980s was a time of major change for the Trump family. In September 1981, Fred Trump Jr. died at age 42 after a long battle with alcoholism. His death profoundly upset Trump, who had avoided consuming

The land for Television City was the largest undeveloped lot in Manhattan. Trump's plan included a 150-story tower. Complaints from neighbors stopped the plan in 1987.

alcohol after seeing its destructive effects on his older brother.

A month later, Ivana and Donald welcomed another Trump into the family. Ivanka Trump was born on October 30, 1981. She was the couple's second child. Eric Trump was born three years later on January 6, 1984.

Ivana with Ivanka, *left*, and Donald Jr., *right*

Donald Jr., Ivanka, and Eric had a sheltered upbringing typical of children in a billionaire family. With Donald and Ivana away making real estate deals and managing jobsites, the children spent much of their time with nannies. The three children were close growing up and remained so as adults.

The Art of the Deal

By 1987, Trump had made multimillion-dollar deals on real estate in New York, New Jersey, and Florida.

He had his own air shuttle service, called Trump Airlines, and lived his business and personal lives in the public eye. The press loved reporting stories of Trump's outrageous lifestyle and business deals. It was an ideal time to release a book cataloging his success.

Trump hired *New York* magazine writer Tony Schwartz to ghostwrite Trump's first book, *The Art of the Deal*. The book describes the details of Trump's most successful business deals. It showcases Trump's public persona, which was brazen, optimistic, and showy. At times, he also had a knack for stretching the truth to make himself look good.

Trump announced the publication of the book on December 12, 1987, with a celebrity-laden party at Trump Tower. *The Art of the Deal* was a hit, remaining on the *New York Times* best seller list for 48 weeks.[8] It exposed Trump and his ideas to the whole country.

Stepping into Politics

Riding high on his success, Trump entered the world of politics. He had worked with the politicians of New York and Atlantic City for more than a decade. In 1987, he considered running in the 1988 presidential election.

To test his support, he took out full-page ads in the *New York Times*, the *Boston Globe*, and the *Washington Post*. In them, Trump offered to negotiate arms deals with the Soviet Union on behalf of President Ronald Reagan. "There's nothing wrong with America's Foreign Defense Policy that a little backbone can't cure," the ads stated.[9]

The ads triggered speculation that Trump was thinking of running for president. Research showed he could be a serious contender in the Republican primary. Trump never formally announced his candidacy, and a speech in New Hampshire was as far as his presidential bid went. But it would not be the last time Trump stood in the political spotlight.

ALL IN THE FAMILY

Trump learned about the real estate business from his father, and he taught his own children in the same way. His three oldest children—Donald Jr., Ivanka, and Eric—became senior executives in Trump's real estate business. As Trump's 2016 bid for president became more serious, his children took on high-profile roles in the campaign. During his presidency, Ivanka worked in the administration as an adviser. "In business and politics, we obviously influence our father's thought process, but he always makes up his own mind," said Donald Jr. "Ivanka, Eric and I have the ability to be very candid with our father."[10]

Trump expanded his brand in many ways, including creating a board game called Trump: The Game in 1989. To play, opponents bid against each other to make real estate deals.

CHAPTER FIVE

BUILDING THE BRAND

An integral part of Trump's success in the 1980s had been his ability to sell himself as a successful real estate developer. As his success grew, he bought a yacht, mansions, limos, and personal jets. His own luxurious lifestyle had become an integral aspect of Trump the businessperson. He had a reputation as one of New York's top real estate developers and richest residents.

The success came at high costs, though. Trump had spent the 1980s acquiring properties to develop. But Trump did not pay for these properties with his own money. He had borrowed hundreds of millions of dollars to fund Trump Tower, the Atlantic City developments, Mar-a-Lago, and the Plaza Hotel. In the 1990s, Trump struggled to repay the money he owed. The next ten years would be tumultuous ones for the New York billionaire.

Trump's luxurious assets, such as helicopters, helped build his reputation of success.

Bankruptcy Hits

Trump's luxurious Taj Mahal casino finally opened in Atlantic City in 1990. It had financial problems from the start. Trump struggled to keep up with the interest payments on the loans that paid for the work on the Taj Mahal.

In December 1990, Trump's father bought 700 poker chips worth $3.5 million at the Taj Mahal. The Casino Control Commission fined the Taj Mahal $65,000 for allowing the purchase.[1] The commission suggested Fred never intended to play the chips. Instead, it alleged the $3.5 million purchase put much-needed cash into the casino's bank account.[2] Fred had, in effect, given the casino an interest-free loan. It violated the casino laws in Atlantic City.

PAYING FOR PROPERTIES

Most real estate developers do not have millions of dollars in cash stored in bank accounts they use to purchase properties. Instead, they rely on loans from big banks to fund their projects. The banks put up their own money to pay for the construction, which the developers pay back over time once their buildings are open for business. Often, cities offer real estate companies incentives for developing properties. Trump received special tax abatements for many of his Manhattan properties, reducing the amount of tax he owed. On high-value properties, abatements can save developers tens of millions of dollars.

In 1991, Trump was fined again. This time it was for giving gifts to a client who played millions of dollars at Trump's casinos. The client was Robert LiButti, an alleged Mafia member. Trump pulled out all the stops for LiButti. He bought LiButti nine luxury cars, including Ferraris, Rolls-Royces, and Bentleys. This violated another casino law, and Trump had to pay $450,000 in fines.[3]

The casino fines added to losses from his airline, hotels, and other investments. Combined with large interest payments, these debts drained Trump's bank accounts. He filed for bankruptcy in 1991. In bankruptcy negotiations, Trump gave up half of his ownership in the Taj Mahal and sold his yacht and Trump Airlines. The bankruptcy deal also forced Trump to follow a personal spending limit, but the Taj Mahal was able to keep its doors open.

The next year, Trump's other casino in Atlantic City, Trump Plaza, put Trump further into debt. It had lost $550 million, and to avoid shutting its doors, Trump once again filed for bankruptcy.[4] In the deal, Trump kept his CEO title but lost his stake in the casino and his salary. After the two bankruptcies, Trump personally owed lenders approximately $900 million.[5]

Throughout the 1980s and 1990s, Trump spent many hours leading board meetings for the companies he owned.

Comeback

Trump later reflected on this difficult time in his book *The Art of the Comeback*. He said he had turned over important decisions to employees. He had pulled back from the day-to-day details of running his business and was no longer using his instincts. As he realized this, he worked to rebuild his business.

In 1993, Trump reassured the press that he had had one of his most successful years ever. Newspapers reported Trump was making a comeback. In 1995, he purchased 40 Wall Street for $1 million.[6] It was a run-down office building in the heart of New York's financial district. After investing $35 million in renovations, the historic building would be worth $500 million 20 years later.[7]

"I got a little cocky and, probably, a little bit lazy. I wasn't working as hard, and I wasn't focusing on the basics. . . . I began to socialize more, probably too much. Frankly, I was bored. I really felt I could do no wrong. Sort of like a baseball player who keeps hitting home runs. . . . My blip—as I call my difficult time—was much different from that of my friends. It was more a sabbatical of sorts. If I'd had my eye on the ball, I'm sure I would have seen more of the problems on the economic horizon."[8]

—Donald Trump,
The Art of the Comeback

But Trump's major success of the 1990s was the renovation at the Penn Central rail yards, where he had once envisioned Television City. To fund the project, Trump made a deal with investors from Hong Kong. The Hong Kong group purchased the property, but Trump would oversee the property's development and lend his name to the project. In 1997, ground broke on the first of seven apartment towers at Trump Place.

Trouble at Home

Just as the 1990s had been a rocky period for his business, Trump's personal life also faced many ups and downs. Trump began a secret affair with model and actress Marla Maples. By Christmas 1989, the secret was out. A few weeks later, Ivana filed for divorce. The press extensively covered their high-profile breakup, which included the division of multimillion-dollar properties and millions in assets.

Trump and Maples married in December 1993 at the Plaza Hotel. Two months earlier, on October 13, they had welcomed a daughter, Tiffany. But the marriage did not last. In 1997, the two announced they were splitting, formally divorcing in 1999. Maples and Tiffany moved to Los Angeles, California, while Trump remained in New

SELLING THE GRAND HYATT

Throughout the boom in the 1980s and the bust of the early 1990s, Trump had kept his 50 percent share of the property that launched his career: the Grand Hyatt. But his partnership with the Hyatt Corporation was always rocky, especially during Trump's 1991 and 1992 bankruptcies. The deteriorating relationship culminated in lawsuits in 1993. In 1996, Trump sold his interest in the Grand Hyatt to the Hyatt Corporation for $140 million. Though he gave up ownership of his first major project, he had turned a profit on his initial $100 million investment.[9]

York. In late 1998, Trump met Slovenian model Melania Knauss at a New York party, and the pair began dating.

In 1999, Trump suffered a personal loss. His father died on June 25 at age 93 after a battle with Alzheimer's disease. Fred left behind an estate worth between $250 million and $300 million.[10] Speaking at his father's funeral, Trump described the day as the toughest of his life.

With the loss of his father, two divorces, and bankruptcy, the 1990s had been challenging years for Trump. But, ever the salesman, he would move forward into the new century promoting his success. A host of new business ventures would cement him as a household name across the United States.

CHAPTER SIX

BRANCHING OUT

As 1999 came to a close, Trump was considering a run for the presidency. Trump's friend Roger Stone, an experienced political adviser, encouraged him. Stone suggested the mood of the country was shifting and that this could be Trump's moment for victory.

The changes had begun seven years earlier. Independent candidate Ross Perot won 19 percent of the votes in the 1992 presidential election.[1] He was a billionaire with no political experience, yet he earned a respectable number of votes. In 1995, he started the Reform Party. Then in 1998, Reform candidate Jesse Ventura was elected governor of Minnesota.

Stone thought Trump could have success with the Reform Party too. In October 1999, Trump joined the Reform Party and launched a bid for the presidency. As time went on, Trump was not confident a Reform Party candidate could win a presidential election. Trump dropped out of the race in February 2000. Though it

Trump appeared on *Larry King Live* to discuss his switch from the Republican Party to the Reform Party on October 7, 1999.

ended quickly, Trump's presidential bid was the first in a series of pursuits outside of real estate.

"You're Fired!"

In 2002, reality television producer Mark Burnett pitched an idea to Trump. Burnett thought Trump's larger-than-life personality could make a business reality show a hit. Trump agreed, and he negotiated a salary of $100,000 per episode and half interest in the show itself.[2] With his name and his business being showcased on every episode, Trump knew the show would help build the Trump brand.

Called *The Apprentice*, Burnett's show pitted contestants against each other for the opportunity to run one of Trump's businesses. Trump was the show's boss, deciding who would continue on and who would be fired. When the show premiered in 2004, it became an instant hit. Millions of viewers tuned in to watch. Charismatic, brazen, and blunt, Trump became a favorite with viewers. He even coined the show's signature catchphrase, "You're fired!"

The Apprentice made Trump a household name nationwide. So did the various spin-off products he licensed in the wake of the show's success. Soon, fans

In the boardroom of *The Apprentice*, Trump, with the help of advisers, decided who would continue to the next episode.

could buy Trump suits and ties, fragrances, and even bottled water. Trump was no longer known as just a real estate developer.

Atlantic City and Chicago

While Trump enjoyed his newfound success as a television personality, all was not well with his real estate investments. Trump's Atlantic City casinos had accumulated $1.8 billion in debt.[3] To avoid collapse, Trump filed for bankruptcy in 2004.

In the proceedings, Trump was able to reduce the interest rates on his debts. He also secured a $500 million loan to improve the properties so they could become more profitable.[4] In return, Trump had to reduce his personal stake in the company to just 25 percent.[5] This meant he no longer had exclusive control over the company. In 2009, Trump was back in bankruptcy court. To save the company, Trump had to resign as chairman of the board.

Never one to be deterred, Trump continued looking for new projects. In 2005, Trump purchased the *Chicago Sun-Times* building in Chicago, Illinois. His renovations transformed it into the city's second-tallest building. Renamed the Trump International Hotel and Tower, it contained condominiums, a luxury hotel, shops, and restaurants.

During these years, Trump was still dating Melania Knauss. The two married on January 22, 2005. They had a glamorous, celebrity-filled reception at Trump's Mar-a-Lago property. The next year, on March 20,

THE CELEBRITY APPRENTICE

In 2007, NBC left *The Apprentice* off of its 2007–2008 schedule, though the network never announced the show had been canceled. The snub upset Trump, who publicly quit the show after the announcement. However, just a few months after the announcement, *The Apprentice*—and its host—were back with a twist. Instead of aspiring businesspeople, the show featured celebrities vying to earn money for a charity of their choice. Trump hosted *The Celebrity Apprentice* through its fourteenth season in 2015. Actor and former governor of California Arnold Schwarzenegger took over as host in 2017 for the fifteenth season.

2006, the Trumps welcomed the birth of their son, Barron.

Trump University

Trump had become a successful real estate developer and television personality, and he had even stepped onto the political stage. In 2005, he rolled out a new venture, Trump University, entering the field of education for the first time.

Trump University courses were intended to help students make money in the real estate industry using Trump's methods. The seminars were taught by instructors the school said Trump had handpicked. The first session was free. Then instructors urged students to purchase a three-day seminar for approximately $1,500 to learn all of Trump's strategies.[6] Next, the instructors offered mentorships to their students for $35,000.[7]

After five years in operation, Trump University was sued by several former students. The students claimed the school was fraudulent. They said its aim was to persuade students to pay thousands of dollars for generic business strategies that had nothing to do with Trump. In the aftermath of the lawsuit, Trump University was forced to change its name to Trump Entrepreneur Initiative. It closed just one year later.

"Birtherism"

In 2011, Trump once again entered the political arena. Trump kicked off an unofficial bid for president by challenging the truth of President Barack Obama's birth certificate. Trump claimed Obama was not born in the United States and was therefore ineligible to be president according to the US Constitution.

THE TROUBLE CONTINUES

The trouble over Trump University continued even after the school closed in 2010. In 2013, New York attorney general Eric Schneiderman filed a lawsuit against Trump. It alleged that the school had misled students in an attempt to make money. In short, the attorney general claimed the school was a fraud. Eventually, in April 2018, the government ordered Trump to pay a $25 million settlement to the students.

While on the 2016 campaign trail, Trump attacked the federal judge presiding over the case, Gonzalo Curiel. Curiel was born in Indiana and is of Mexican heritage. Trump accused Curiel of bias in the case because he was of Mexican heritage—Trump had plans to build a wall along the US–Mexico border.

The comment sparked outrage in the media and among voters and dozens of politicians, Republican and Democratic alike. At first, Trump defended his statement. But it hurt him in the polls. After the attack, approximately 64 percent of Americans believed Trump was unfit to be president.[8] Trump later distanced himself from the issue.

This theory became known as "birtherism," with proponents known as "birthers." Trump demanded Obama present his birth certificate as proof that he was born in the United States. At first, Obama dismissed Trump and the birthers. But Trump continued pressing the president on the issue. He appeared on morning talk shows to discuss his theory and repeat his demand that Obama make his birth certificate public.

The more Trump pushed the birth issue, the higher he rose in opinion polling about potential Republican candidates. At one point, he had nearly reached the top. In April, after six weeks of demands, Trump finally got his wish. President Obama released a copy of his birth certificate that showed he was born in Honolulu, Hawaii.

Over the next month, Trump's polling numbers started to sink. By mid-May, more than 60 percent of those polled disapproved of him.[9] On May 16, Trump formally announced that he would not run for president. "The decision does not come easily or without regret," he said. "I maintain the strong conviction that if I were to run, I would be able to win the primary and ultimately, the general election," he added.[10] In four years, he would try his hand again.

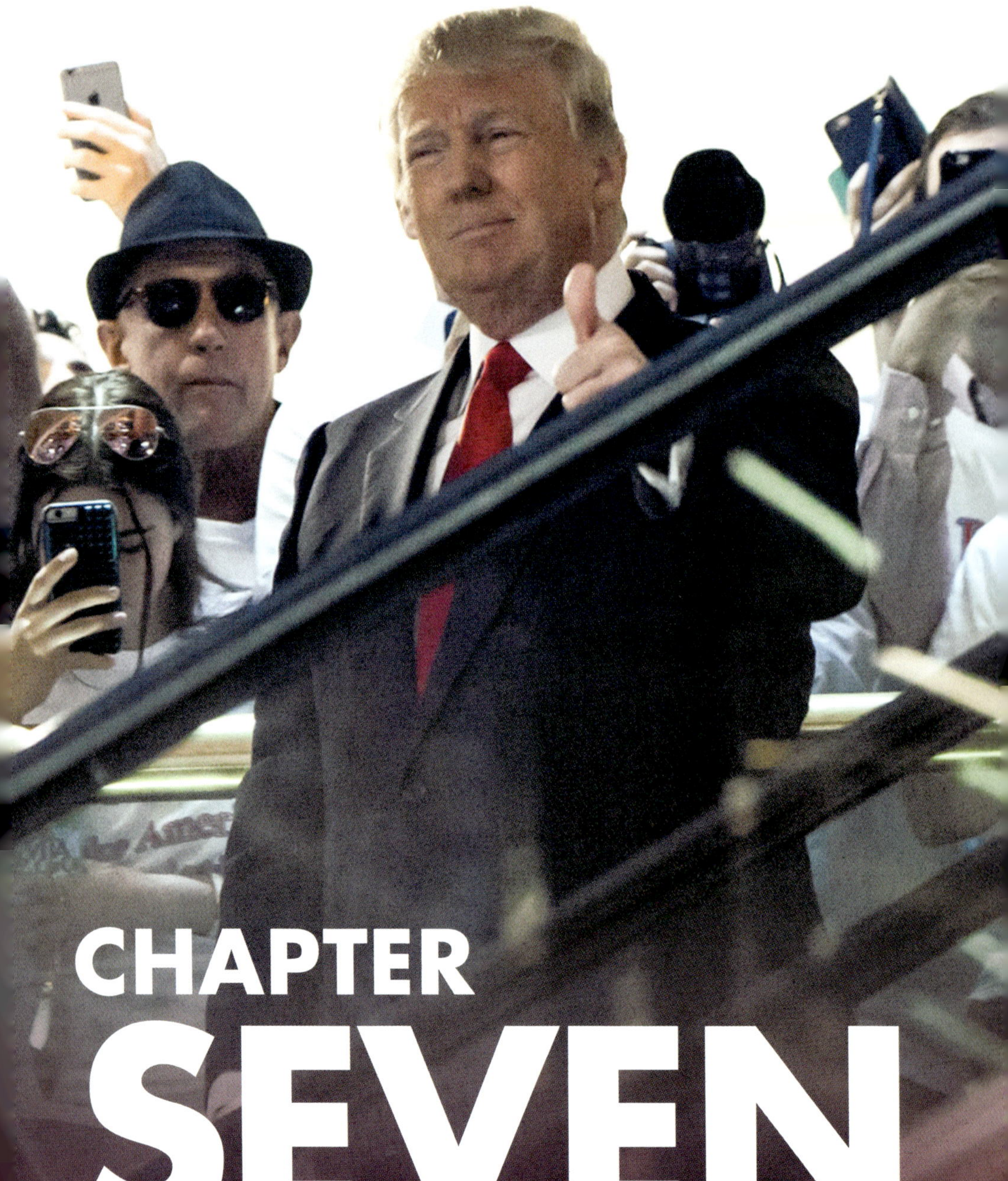

CHAPTER SEVEN

MAKE AMERICA GREAT AGAIN

On June 16, 2015, Trump descended the escalator at Trump Tower to a waiting crowd in the skyscraper's lobby. He announced that he was officially running for president of the United States. He promised to use his business know-how to improve the country. And he said he would fund his own campaign.

"Our country needs a truly great leader, and we need a truly great leader now," Trump told the crowd. "Sadly, the American dream is dead. But if I get elected president I will bring it back bigger and better and stronger than ever before, and we will make America great again."[1]

The tone of Trump's speech reflected his aggressive style. He hit hard against President Obama and promised to repeal Obama's health care reform law, the Affordable Care Act. Trump also spoke forcefully about trade, terrorism, and immigration.

Trump's thumbs-up was a signature move during his campaign.

Trump's comments about immigration drew harsh criticism. He said Mexico was sending immigrants who were violent criminals to the United States. He discussed his idea for a wall along the US–Mexico border to keep people from crossing unlawfully, adding that he would make Mexico pay for it.

Clinching the Nomination

In his quest for the Republican nomination, Trump had 16 rivals. It was the largest field of candidates for one party in modern history. Trump aimed verbal attacks against his opponents and made up disparaging

TRUMP AND THE PRESS

Throughout his campaign, Trump had a complicated relationship with the national press. As he did as a businessperson, Trump used coverage from the media to communicate his positions and agenda. His experience as a television host made him an engaging and entertaining subject. By March 15, 2016, experts calculated that Trump had received nearly $2 billion in free media coverage in his campaign. That was more than six times the amount of Ted Cruz, his closest rival in the Republican primary race.[2]

Though he enjoyed regular interviews and intense coverage of his rallies, Trump took a hard line against what he saw as a media bias against him and his supporters. He insulted and sometimes threatened journalists who challenged him on his positions during press conferences. He banned several news organizations from attending his campaign events. Trump also vowed that as president, he would change the nation's laws to make it easier to sue newspapers for "purposely negative" articles.[3]

nicknames for them. Some of these attacks were made on the primary debate stage, but many others were made in press interviews, at campaign rallies, and on Trump's preferred social media platform, Twitter.

Trump's inflammatory rhetoric resonated with many Americans. Supporters appreciated his bluntness. They felt Trump was unafraid to say what they believed to be true on issues such as law enforcement, immigration, and the economy. This style won Trump state after state in the primaries, and by May 2016 he had become the presumptive nominee.

> *"One thing I've learned about the press is that they're always hungry for a good story, and the more sensational the better. . . . The point is that if you are a little different, or a little outrageous, or if you do things that are bold and controversial, the press is going to write about you. I've always done things a little differently, I don't mind controversy, and my deals tend to be somewhat ambitious. . . . The result is that the press has always wanted to write about me."[4]*
>
> *—Donald Trump,*
> The Art of the Deal

Defining Positions on Trade and Treaties

Trump said little about his foreign policy plans during the early part of his campaign, but he stated that "'America First' will be the major and overriding theme of my administration."[5] As Trump began campaigning for the general election, he rolled out proposals for changing trade deals and defense treaties. Trump promised to throw out the Trans-Pacific Partnership (TPP) deal President Obama had negotiated with countries in the Americas and East Asia. He also planned to renegotiate the North American Free Trade Agreement (NAFTA), a part of US trade policy since 1994. Doing so, he explained, would keep more jobs in the United States.

Trump also said he would renegotiate defense treaties. The most notable of these involved the North Atlantic Treaty Organization (NATO). The United States was a founding member of NATO in 1949 and had been part of the organization ever since. Trump argued that the United States contributed much more to

"LOCK HER UP!"

Trump and the Republican Party spent much of the Republican National Convention making the case for why the presumptive Democratic nominee, Hillary Clinton, was unfit to be president. On the second night, New Jersey governor Chris Christie took the stage as the crowds chanted, "Lock her up!"[6] He disparaged Clinton's work as secretary of state. Her handling of classified information on a private email server set up in her home became the focus of intense criticism, as did her leadership in the wake of an attack on US diplomats in Benghazi, Libya. These criticisms would remain talking points through the rest of the election.

In his speech at the 2016 Republican National Convention in Cleveland, Ohio, Trump spoke about law and order, as well as the "forgotten men and women" of the country.

NATO than other members. He said he would get the United States a better deal.

On July 15, Trump officially announced Indiana governor Mike Pence as his running mate. Governor Pence was a social conservative with a long career in politics and a calm personality. Advisers believed he was a good complement to Trump's bombastic personality and lack of political experience. A few days later, Republicans formally nominated Trump as the nominee for president and Pence as the nominee for vice president at the Republican National Convention.

Trump had won the primary contest. The next step was the presidential election.

Tied in the Polls

After the convention, Trump enjoyed a bump in the polls. But next came the Democratic Party's turn. Over the four days of the Democratic National Convention, party members, including President Barack Obama and Vice President Joe Biden, endorsed Hillary Clinton. She officially became the party nominee—and the first major party female presidential nominee in US history—on July 26.

Speakers at the convention outlined their case against a Trump presidency. Some said Trump's personality made him unfit to be president. Clinton and others asserted that Trump's vision of the United States did not fit the ideals of the nation.

Like Trump, Clinton enjoyed a bump in the polls following the party convention. But the increased support did not last. Over August and September, Trump chipped away at Clinton's lead. By the time of the first presidential debate in September, polls indicated the candidates were very close.

Trump and Clinton Take the Stage

Trump and Clinton faced off on the debate stage for the first time on September 26. Historically, presidential candidates spend weeks preparing for the debate, reading up on the issues and preparing arguments against opponents' talking points. This was the approach Clinton took leading up to September 26, but Trump was an unconventional candidate. He was confident that his experience speaking on television and at rallies would be enough preparation.

Throughout the debate, Clinton answered questions regarding the economy, national security, and foreign policy. Trump spent much of the debate criticizing Clinton and

THE *ACCESS HOLLYWOOD* TAPE

On October 7, 2016, an 11-year-old tape of an unaired *Access Hollywood* TV show segment surfaced. The tape caught Trump having a lewd conversation about women with the show's host. The content of the tape was shocking and offensive to many voters and Republican officials. Trump apologized for his comments. He also asserted to Hillary Clinton that her husband, former president Bill Clinton, had treated women much worse. Over the next few days, nearly 20 percent of Republican governors and Republican members of Congress withdrew their support of Trump.[7] Some went so far as to call for Trump to step down as the presidential nominee. But Trump refused to do so.

defending himself. He frequently lost focus on the topic at hand.

Trump also used this approach for the second and third debates. In polling by the analytics company Gallup, viewers chose Clinton as the winner of the three debates by wide margins. It was unclear what effect this would have on the election.

Election Day 2016

On November 7, the day before the US presidential election, most polls favored Clinton. But the Trump campaign remained cautiously optimistic about its chances. Throughout the election season, Trump had defied expectations. From the morning he announced his candidacy, political experts had predicted Trump would not be successful. But he had beaten his Republican rivals during the primary season, mobilizing a base of voters who felt politicians did not represent them, disagreed with the path the country was on, and demanded change.

On November 8, Americans cast their votes for president. As election results poured in, it became clear that while polls and political experts had been right about Clinton's lead in the popular vote, Trump was

Trump shook hands with excited supporters at an election night rally in 2016.

winning the states he needed to claim victory. Most states give all their electoral votes to the popular vote winner within the state, and it's possible to win the election with fewer direct votes by winning the right states. Shortly after Trump reached the 270 electoral votes required to win, Clinton called him to concede the election. Clinton ultimately won the national popular vote by about 2.8 million votes. Trump became the president-elect of the United States.[8]

CHAPTER EIGHT

PRESIDENT TRUMP

Hundreds of thousands of spectators stood before the West Front of the US Capitol on January 20, 2017, to witness Trump's presidential inauguration. Millions more watched the event on television. After taking the oath of office, Trump gave his first speech as president. He spoke directly to the American people, saying, "I will fight for you with every breath in my body, and I will never, ever let you down."[1] Trump made many promises during his campaign. Now that he was president, he set about trying to fulfill them.

Domestic Policies

Undocumented immigration was one of Trump's top domestic priorities. Shortly after taking office, he issued an executive order that called for undocumented residents to be deported and for the building of more detention centers along the US–Mexico border. The order also called for the building of his promised wall along the southern border.

With his hand on a Bible held by his wife, Melania, Trump took the oath of office on January 20, 2017.

On January 27, Trump issued an executive order banning people from seven mostly Muslim countries from visiting the United States for 90 days. Many critics saw this as a follow-up on his campaign promise to ban Muslims from coming to the country. With both the campaign promise and the executive order, Trump said the aim was to curb terrorism. Within a few days, court challenges stopped the enforcement of the order pending litigation. In March, Trump issued a modified travel ban. Legal challenges over these efforts would continue for the next few years.

Deregulation was another priority. Trump ordered the removal of many regulations in an effort to cut government spending and promote business growth. This included many environmental rules.

TRUMP AND THE ENVIRONMENT

Trump's efforts to decrease government regulations and increase economic growth were often criticized by environmentalists. His administration loosened regulations on air and water quality, fuel economy, and animal protection, and it opened public land for mining and drilling, including in national parks and wildlife refuges. Many businesses supported these changes, since they reduced costs. In one of his most dramatic moves, Trump announced his intention to withdraw the United States from the Paris Climate Agreement—an international, voluntary agreement aimed at reducing greenhouse gas emissions that contribute to climate change.

In November 2017, the Trump administration unveiled the Tax Cuts and Jobs Act, legislation meant to spur economic growth using major tax cuts. Personal tax rates for most Americans decreased, and the corporate tax rate was cut sharply, a move intended to encourage companies to invest in their businesses and workers. The tax cuts decreased government revenue. Proponents of the bill said that increased economic activity would provide additional tax revenue that would offset the cost of the tax cuts.

Political Appointments

Federal judicial appointments, such as district court judges, court of appeals judges, and Supreme Court justices, are among the most important presidential appointees. Federal judges are appointed for life, and they can affect political matters long after a president has left office. But as a check to this power, the president's choices have to be approved by the Senate. Senate majority leader Mitch McConnell, a Republican, worked to confirm as many of Trump's judicial nominees as possible. In the spring of 2020, the final year of Trump's presidency, McConnell said, "My motto for the year is 'leave no vacancy behind.'"[2]

Appointing Brett Kavanaugh, *far left*, and Neil Gorsuch, *second from left*, to the Supreme Court were key achievements of Trump's presidency.

During his presidency, Trump appointed three Supreme Court justices—Neil Gorsuch, Brett Kavanaugh, and Amy Coney Barrett. Confirmation of Gorsuch and Kavanaugh didn't come easily. Trump nominated Gorsuch to fill a justice seat made available during the Obama presidency. Justice Antonin Scalia died in February 2016, and Obama nominated Merrick Garland to replace him. Republicans blocked the seat from being filled until after that fall's election, angering Democrats. Then, to confirm Gorsuch, Republicans amended Senate rules so that a simple majority was enough to confirm judicial nominees, rather than 60 votes. Kavanaugh's confirmation was plagued by controversy after multiple women accused him of sexual abuse. He denied the allegations, and the Senate confirmed his appointment to the Supreme Court after a highly publicized hearing. Trump nominated Amy Coney Barrett following the September 2020 death of Justice Ruth Bader Ginsburg. Barrett was confirmed by the Senate on October 27.

Foreign Policy

The US president is the commander-in-chief of the armed forces and interacts frequently with other heads of state, making him or her central to US foreign policy. There were many looming foreign policy issues when Trump became president, including a war in Afghanistan that had been ongoing since 2001, a fight against the Islamic State in Iraq and Syria (ISIS) terrorist group in Iraq, and tensions with Iran.

Trump had said little about the war in Afghanistan during his election campaign. In August 2017, he announced a policy regarding the conflict. His policy called for continued support of the Afghan government and military, a crackdown on countries providing support and safe haven to terrorist organizations, and increased contributions from allied countries.

In March 2020, the United States signed a peace deal with the Taliban, a militant group in conflict with the Afghan government. In the deal, the United States agreed to begin withdrawing military forces. Though conflict between the Taliban and Afghan forces continued, the deal was a significant milestone in the effort to end the war.

Trump's policies concerning Iraq were centered around defeating ISIS forces in the country, but these efforts became linked with Iran and Syria as the complex political and military situation evolved. The United States had been battling ISIS in Syria since 2014. In December 2018, Trump claimed victory over ISIS in Syria, and he ordered the withdrawal of US forces from the country. In February 2019, Trump agreed to keep a

NORTH KOREA

Before he left office, President Obama warned Trump that one of his greatest foreign policy challenges would be North Korea's nuclear weapons program. By 2017, the country was actively testing nuclear weapons and the missiles that could carry them long distances. For more than a year, Trump and North Korean leader Kim Jong-un fought a war of words over the issue of denuclearization. Then, in March 2018, Kim reached out to Trump, inviting him to meet to discuss the issue. Trump and Kim eventually met in person three times. Though no deals were made, Trump would later say that his leadership had prevented a war with North Korea. North Korea continued to develop and display new missiles in 2020.

small peacekeeping force of soldiers in Syria, but he said that it wasn't a reversal of his previous withdrawal order.

In his 2015 speech announcing his presidential campaign, Trump had called out Iran as a particular threat. At the time, the United States, along with several other countries, was negotiating a deal with Iran. Iran would limit its nuclear weapons program in exchange for other nations lifting sanctions against it. This became the Iran Nuclear Agreement, which went into effect in January 2016. Trump didn't believe Iran would honor the agreement and felt that it failed to protect the United States and its allies. On May 8, 2018, Trump announced that the United States was withdrawing from the agreement and was restarting sanctions. As a result, Iran began resuming its nuclear program. Tensions escalated.

Over the course of the next year, Iran attacked and seized foreign ships in the Persian Gulf, and Iran-backed rebels launched attacks in Iraq and Saudi Arabia. Then in January 2020, Trump ordered an air strike outside of Baghdad, Iraq, that killed top Iranian general Qasem Soleimani. Iran struck back, launching missile attacks against two US military bases in Iraq that wounded several soldiers. After these events, both Trump and Iran backed down, as neither wanted an all-out war.

Flanked by his national security team, Trump addressed the nation from the White House on January 8, 2020, regarding the quickly rising tensions with Iran.

In September 2020, Trump celebrated a significant diplomatic achievement. Two Arab nations in the Middle East, Bahrain and the United Arab Emirates, agreed to officially recognize Israel and open diplomatic relations with the country. Israel had long experienced tensions and conflict with its neighbors, so this event was a major breakthrough. The leaders of the three nations met at the White House to sign the official agreements. At the meeting, Trump said, "After decades of division and conflict we mark the dawn of a new Middle East."[3]

Trade Policies

Trade was an important issue to Trump. In his 2020 State of the Union address, he said, "Unfair trade is perhaps the single biggest reason that I decided to run for president."[4] During his campaign, Trump had promised to crack down on what he called unfair trade practices by China. These included industrial subsidies, intellectual property theft, and dumping, which is the practice of exporting goods at artificially low prices to drive out competitors. In January 2018, Trump imposed the first of a series of tariffs on China, sparking a trade war between the two countries. Both nations placed tariffs on tens of billions of dollars' worth of imported food, raw materials, and goods.

While the government collected billions of dollars in tariffs and domestic businesses received some protection from foreign competitors, critics contended that the money came at the expense of American importers, who paid the tariffs, and American consumers, who had to pay higher prices for goods. The trade war hit American farmers especially hard, prompting Trump's administration to provide them with $28 billion in aid.[5] In early December 2018, Trump and China's president,

Trump and Xi met in Beijing, China, in November 2017. Economic tensions between the two nations continued through most of Trump's presidency.

Xi Jinping, began negotiations to end the trade war. In 2019, they reached an agreement to reduce tariffs and resolve trade disputes.

Personal Ethics

When Trump was elected, he vowed not to take the $400,000 annual presidential salary. He donated the equivalent amount to a variety of government agencies each year. Trump did make money in another way. While president, Trump often housed government employees at his resorts and hotels at taxpayer expense.

He did not disconnect from his private businesses, which presidents usually did to prevent conflicts of interest.

In addition, during his presidency Trump was accused by at least 17 women of inappropriate sexual behavior that had allegedly occurred before his election. Two of these women sought legal action against him while he was in office.[6]

The Mueller Report

During the 2016 presidential campaign, Russian agents hacked the Democratic National Committee and the Hillary Clinton campaign, and they leaked politically damaging information on the internet in an attempt to help Trump get elected.[7] This prompted an FBI investigation in the summer of 2016. In part, the investigation looked into alleged collusion between the Trump campaign and Russia.

On May 9, 2017, President Trump fired FBI director James Comey, who later said the move was an attempt to end the investigation. The Trump administration said top officials suggested Trump fire Comey. Deputy Attorney General Rod Rosenstein then appointed former FBI director Robert Mueller as special counsel to continue the investigation. Mueller was given broad authority to examine any crimes discovered during the probe. Trump frequently referred to the Mueller investigation as a "witch hunt."[8]

Mueller's investigation lasted 22 months, during which time he and his team conducted approximately 500 interviews and charged 34 people with crimes, including businesspeople, campaign staffers, and Russian intelligence officers.[9] Mueller released a 448-page report of his findings in April 2019. The investigation found far-reaching Russian attempts to influence the 2016 election. It did not find evidence that the Trump campaign knowingly colluded with the Russians.

Trouble at the Border

Trump's plan for protecting the US–Mexico border was to add border security agents, strengthen immigration laws, and build a border wall. One of his first acts as president was to sign an executive order to begin the process of building the wall. But actually building and paying for it proved to be difficult. Trump had promised during his campaign that Mexico would pay for the wall, but Mexico refused. Trump sought alternate ways to fund it.

On April 6, 2018, Attorney General Jeff Sessions announced the administration's new zero tolerance policy on undocumented immigration, in which every person caught crossing the border illegally would be detained and prosecuted. As a result of this policy, parents and children were separated, because children were not allowed in the federal prisons where their parents were being held. In six weeks, more than 2,000 children were separated from their families.[10] The separations were traumatic for both children and adults. Politicians, the public, and the international community fiercely criticized this effect of the zero tolerance policy, which prompted Trump to alter the policy and end the separation of children on June 20, 2018. Shortly after, a federal judge ordered the families to be reunited.

THE BORDER WALL

When Trump was unable to get funds for the US–Mexico border wall from Congress, he threatened to shut down the government. Trump made good on his threat. On December 22, 2018, the government partially shut down when Trump declined to sign a 2019 government funding bill that didn't include money for the wall. Both sides dug in. Trump was determined to get the funds, and Congress said no. Trump relented on January 25, agreeing to a short-term bill that would fund the government long enough for a deal to be reached. At 35 days, the government shutdown was the longest in US history.[11]

CHAPTER NINE

A TUMULTUOUS FINAL YEAR

During a July 25, 2019, phone call with newly elected Ukrainian president Volodymyr Zelensky, Trump asked Zelensky to investigate former vice president Joe Biden and Biden's son, Hunter. In 2014, Hunter had joined the board of a Ukrainian natural gas company called Burisma. In 2016, Joe Biden pushed for the firing of Ukrainian prosecutor general Viktor Shokin for corruption, holding up US aid to Ukraine until that happened. After getting fired, Shokin suggested he had been removed for investigating Burisma. Trump referred to this situation in the call.

It was later discovered that a week before the call, Trump had ordered the withholding of congressionally approved military aid to Ukraine. Democrats accused Trump of using the aid as leverage to force Zelensky to conduct an investigation. Both Trump and Zelensky stated there was no such exchange of favors. Trump

Trump and his public health team spoke at a February 26, 2020, press conference at the White House.

said the money was held over concerns of corruption in Ukraine.

EXPOSING CORRUPTION

Whistleblowers are integral parts of fighting government corruption and exposing wrongdoing that often occurs away from the public eye. Their identities are often unknown except to a select few. Trump's impeachment inquiry was sparked by the complaint of an unknown whistleblower. Republicans tried to learn the individual's identity, but whistleblowers' identities are protected by the Whistleblower Protection Act, which is intended to shield them from retaliation.

In August, a whistleblower in the US government filed a complaint concerning the July 25 phone call. The whistleblower expressed concern that Trump had used the call to undermine Biden, a likely 2020 presidential election rival, using foreign help. This prompted Congress to launch an official impeachment inquiry into Trump. Impeachment is a power granted by the US Constitution allowing Congress to remove government officials from office. Trump called the inquiry a "hoax" meant to overturn the 2016 presidential election, and he announced that his administration would not cooperate.[1]

The impeachment inquiry lasted more than two months, and it included testimonies from dozens of government officials. On December 18, members of the House cast their votes on whether to impeach Trump on two articles—abuse of power and obstruction of Congress. Members voted mostly along party lines, which ensured impeachment in the Democrat-led House. Trump was the third impeached president in US history.

An impeachment only levels charges against a president. Next, the Republican-led Senate would hold an impeachment trial. A two-thirds majority in the Senate would convict the president and remove him from office. Some Republican senators announced before the trial that they would vote to acquit.

Opening arguments began on January 22. For three days, House Democrats presented evidence from the impeachment inquiry and argued that it warranted Trump's removal from office. The defense team then spent three days responding. The team argued that Trump was simply exercising his powers as president, and that even if Trump had done what Democrats accused him of, that would not merit removal.

Amid this, Trump gave his State of the Union address on February 4. The impeachment trial vote was the next day. Senators voted almost entirely along party lines, and Trump was acquitted on both articles. Senator Mitt Romney was the only Republican to vote guilty

Speaker of the House Nancy Pelosi presided over the impeachment vote in the House of Representatives.

on either charge, voting to convict Trump for abuse of power. Speaking from the White House the day after his acquittal, Trump applauded the work done by his defense team and Republican senators and reaffirmed his innocence.

Pandemic

In early January 2020, Trump began receiving warnings from intelligence officials of a dangerous new virus making people sick in China. The virus was part of a family of viruses called coronaviruses. It caused a deadly infectious disease called COVID-19. On January 21, health authorities announced the first confirmed case in the United States. In the following days and weeks, Trump created the Coronavirus Task Force and began restricting international travel. But by late February, the aggressive virus had spread throughout the United States and numerous other countries. While medical experts called for the government to take more action to contain the virus, Trump downplayed the severity of the crisis. At a February 27 press conference, he said, "It's going to disappear. One day it's like a miracle, it will disappear."[2]

In March, Trump and the rest of the government increased the federal response to the virus. On March 6, he signed an emergency bill appropriating $8.3 billion to combat the coronavirus in the United States, and on March 13, he declared a national emergency, two days after the World Health Organization (WHO) declared that COVID-19 had become a global pandemic.

Also in March, state governments began issuing mandatory stay-at-home orders that required workers other than essential personnel, such as hospital workers and grocery store employees, to remain at home. Schools, stores, restaurants, theaters, concert halls, and sports venues shut down to avoid spreading the virus. Millions of people were suddenly out of work. Applications for unemployment skyrocketed, and the stock market plummeted. On March 27, Trump signed the largest stimulus package in US history—the Coronavirus Aid, Relief, and Economic Security

(CARES) Act, which provided $2 trillion to support hospitals, develop vaccines, keep businesses afloat, and provide Americans with direct payments to help boost the economy.

While the government fought to get the pandemic under control, Trump was criticized by the media, politicians, and medical experts for his handling of the crisis. Many considered his response time too slow and felt that his predictions for a quick recovery and speedy vaccine production were unrealistic. He came under particular criticism for promoting unproven drug treatments. For his part, Trump praised his handling of the crisis. After initially praising China and the WHO for their response, he began sharply criticizing them in April, stating that they had misled the world on the dangers of the virus.

Coronavirus cases continued to rise throughout the summer. When Trump and congressional Democrats failed to reach an agreement on the contents of a new aid package in early August, Trump used his executive powers to provide unemployment benefits and tax incentives for businesses, for temporary relief until an agreement was reached. The pandemic dominated the remainder of Trump's term in office, as he struggled to find a balance between keeping people safe and rebuilding the economy. In September, the US death toll from the virus crossed 200,000. Millions more had become ill and recovered.

Friday, October 2, brought a shocking development. Trump and the First Lady both tested positive for COVID-19, as did a large cluster of White House staff, political and military leaders, and journalists. All had recently attended White House events.

Due to his age and underlying health conditions, Trump was at high risk for poor outcomes of COVID-19. On Friday his doctors gave him supplemental oxygen and experimental drugs. They brought him to Walter Reed Military Medical Center that evening. He remained there over the weekend, returning to the White House

STRUGGLING TO REOPEN

In the spring of 2020, Trump sought to reopen the country, which had been in lockdown due to the coronavirus pandemic. State governors have the right to implement their own safety rules, and some thought it was too soon to reopen. They wanted to protect people in their states and refused to follow any directives from the president that might put them in danger. Trump stated in an April interview that he had total authority as president to reopen cities and states, which prompted a heated argument with state leaders and legal experts over the extent of presidential authority.

on Monday. He tweeted, “Feeling really good! Don’t be afraid of COVID. Don’t let it dominate your life.”[3]

Protests against Police Brutality

On May 25, 2020, an unarmed Black man named George Floyd died following an encounter with a white police officer and three other officers in Minneapolis, Minnesota. Afterward, protests were held throughout the country. Rioting and looting took place in several cities. Trump demanded an aggressive crackdown on protesting and suggested in a tweet that law enforcement could shoot when dealing with looters. Protests and riots continued throughout the summer as other instances of police brutality against Black Americans occurred.

TRUMP AND TWITTER

Trump is an avid user of Twitter, a social media platform that lets users send short messages to their followers. Twitter has transformed the way many Americans discuss politics and follow elections. It gives citizens direct, unfiltered access to candidates and officials. During Trump’s first three years in office, he tweeted more than 11,000 times.[4]

Many Americans called for the reform of police departments, including shifting police resources to other services, to help curb police brutality. Trump felt it was important to be tough on crime, and he proposed to substantially increase police funding to combat the problem. Trump blamed state and local governments led by Democrats for allowing the riots to take place.

Reelection Campaign

Trump officially announced his 2020 reelection campaign at a rally in Orlando, Florida, on June 18, 2019. As an incumbent candidate, Trump easily secured the Republican nomination during the 2020 primary elections. On the Democratic side, Biden clinched the party nomination after his last major rival dropped out of the race in April 2020.

The pandemic put a stop to Trump's traditional campaign rallies for several months. He began a virtual campaign with daily videos posted online. He held his first rally in months in Tulsa, Oklahoma, on June 20. Some people, including the director of the Tulsa Health Department, suggested that the rally played a role in Tulsa's later surge in COVID-19 cases. The campaign canceled a planned follow-up rally in New Hampshire. Trump's large-scale rallies, now held outdoors and mostly at airports, resumed in August.

Run-Up to the Election

On September 27, the *New York Times* published a story revealing that because of reported business losses, Trump had paid little or no federal income tax in the preceding 15 years. It also explained that he was hundreds of millions of dollars in debt. Following publication of the story, many people criticized Trump for paying less in income tax than many less-well-off Americans. Some also suggested national security concerns, saying that a president deeply in debt could be subject to foreign influence. Trump described the *Times* story as "made up" and "fake news."[5]

The presidential debates, often contentious events, were particularly heated. The first was held on September 29. Trump was aggressive in the debate, frequently interrupting Biden and moderator Chris Wallace of Fox News. Biden criticized the Trump administration's handling of the pandemic. For his part, Trump pointed to the strong economy in the months before the pandemic. The second debate, planned for October 15, was canceled following Trump's COVID-19 diagnosis.

More than 60 million people watched the final 2020 presidential debate on television.

It wasn't until October 22 that another debate took place. Trump, having recovered from his case of COVID-19, met Biden face-to-face in Nashville, Tennessee. But the rules were different this time. Because of Trump's interruptions during the last debate, the debate organizers decided to turn off each candidate's microphone when the other gave his opening remarks. The result was a much calmer debate.

Election Day 2020

Election Day was November 3. Polling suggested that Biden was leading nationally by double digits and more narrowly in the key swing states. He hoped for a landslide victory. But as in 2016, some of the polls proved to be wrong. Voters turned out in record numbers, and the two candidates were neck and neck in several key battleground states. The day ended without a clear winner.

Millions of mail-in ballots remained to be counted, and this task would take several days. Many of those ballots were expected to be for Biden. Polling showed that Democrats were more likely to vote by mail, in part because Trump had discouraged people from voting by mail, suggesting this method was prone to voter fraud. The day after the election, Trump declared: "This is an embarrassment to our country. We were getting ready to win this election. Frankly, we did win this election."[6] The Trump campaign sued several states to stop them from counting mail-in ballots. Despite these efforts, the counting continued. Biden's lead began to grow in key states. On November 7, when Biden took a clear lead in Pennsylvania, major news organizations projected he would win its 20 electoral votes, bringing him to the 270 electoral votes needed to clinch the election. They declared him the president-elect.

On the night of November 5, Trump gave a press conference in which he claimed to have won the election.

A New Chapter

Trump contested the election results. In the following weeks, lawyers filed lawsuits claiming voter fraud. The suits were dismissed. As states began to certify their election results, lawyers continued their legal claims but failed to change the election's outcome. On November 23, the Trump administration officially began the transition process.

Trump left office on January 20, 2021, moving on to the next chapter of his life. During his administration he faced many challenges, such as impeachment and a global pandemic. But his many accomplishments included the CARES Act and historic agreements in the Middle East. He made history as a businessperson, TV personality, and US president.

TIMELINE

1946

Donald John Trump is born on June 14 in Jamaica Estates, Queens, New York City.

1968

Trump graduates from the Wharton School of Business at the University of Pennsylvania on May 20.

1977

On April 9, Trump marries Ivana Winklmayr; their son, Donald John Trump Jr., is born on December 31.

1981

Ivanka Trump is born on October 30.

1982

Trump Tower is completed in Manhattan.

1984

Eric Trump is born on January 6.

1990
Ivana and Trump announce they are divorcing.

1991
Trump files for bankruptcy following significant losses from his casinos, hotels, airline, and other investments.

1993
Tiffany Trump is born on October 13; Trump marries Marla Maples in December.

1999
Trump and Maples formally divorce; Fred Trump dies at age 93 on June 25.

2004
Trump's hit reality television show *The Apprentice* premieres.

2005
Trump marries Melania Knauss on January 22.

2006
Barron Trump is born on March 20.

TIMELINE

2015

Trump announces his candidacy for president of the United States on June 16.

2016

Trump becomes the official Republican nominee for president in July, and he is elected the forty-fifth president on November 8.

2017

Trump is inaugurated at the US Capitol on January 20; he issues a travel ban executive order on January 27; after legal challenges, he issues a revised ban in March; Trump's administration reveals the Tax Cuts and Jobs Act in November.

2018

In March, Trump begins a peace-seeking dialogue with North Korean leader Kim Jong-un; in April, Attorney General Jeff Sessions announces the administration's zero tolerance policy on undocumented immigration; the resulting family separations are highly controversial.

2019

In April, Robert Mueller releases his report on an investigation into Russian interference in the 2016 election; in July, Trump has a phone call with the Ukrainian president that eventually leads to Trump's impeachment on December 18.

2020

On February 5, Trump is acquitted in his impeachment trial; the COVID-19 pandemic sickens millions of Americans and kills hundreds of thousands; Trump signs the CARES Act in March to support businesses and individuals in the pandemic; in September, Trump hosts leaders from the United Arab Emirates, Bahrain, and Israel as they sign historic diplomatic agreements; in October, Trump contracts COVID-19 and recovers; on November 3, Trump loses his reelection bid to Democratic challenger Joe Biden.

ESSENTIAL FACTS

Date of Birth

June 14, 1946

Place of Birth

Jamaica Estates, Queens, New York

Parents

Fred Trump and Mary Anne Trump

Education

New York Military Academy; Fordham University; University of Pennsylvania's Wharton School of Business

Marriages

Ivana Winklmayr (1977–1990), Marla Maples (1993–1999), Melania Knauss (2005–)

Children

Donald Jr., Ivanka, Eric, Tiffany, Barron

Career Highlights

Trump's career began with real estate development in New York City, New York, including the Commodore Hotel and Trump Tower. In the early 1980s, Trump opened three large luxury casinos in Atlantic City, New Jersey. In 2016, he was elected forty-fifth president of the United States.

Societal Contributions

Trump renovated buildings in New York City, revitalizing the surrounding neighborhoods and providing jobs for thousands during the projects. As president, he signed large tax cuts into law, helping to stimulate economic growth. He oversaw the nation's response to the coronavirus pandemic.

Conflicts

In 1973, Trump's company faced a lawsuit for violating the Fair Housing Act. The lawsuit was settled, stating the company did not commit any wrongdoing.

On the campaign trail, Trump's proposals to ban Muslim immigration and build a wall on the US-Mexico border were met with criticism. Tapes of Trump making lewd comments about women drew the anger of Republicans and Democrats alike.

Robert Mueller investigated whether Trump's campaign had colluded with Russia in the 2016 election; the resulting report found no evidence of collusion. In 2019, Trump was impeached and later acquitted regarding a phone call with the Ukrainian president.

Quote

"I am thrilled to report to you tonight that our economy is the best it has ever been. . . . Our borders are secure. Our families are flourishing. Our values are renewed. Our pride is restored." —*Donald Trump, State of the Union address, 2020*

GLOSSARY

abatement
A deduction.

asset
An item of value.

conservative
Believing in small government and established social, economic, and political traditions and practices.

draft
A system in which people of a certain age are required to register for military service.

ghostwrite
To write for someone else who is the assumed author.

interest
A fee charged when a person or business borrows money, or money paid to people as an incentive for keeping their money in a bank.

liberal
Believing in large government and supporting new ideas and ways of behaving.

lobbyist
Someone who tries to convince government officials to vote in a certain way as part of his or her job.

majority share

The ownership of more than half a company, giving the owner a degree of control or influence over that company.

pandemic

The worldwide spread of a disease.

presumptive

Probable.

primary

A contest political parties hold to determine their presidential nominees.

rhetoric

Language intended to influence people, even if it may not be completely truthful.

zoning

The government's division of a city or town into separate areas designated for specific purposes, such as residential or commercial use.

ADDITIONAL RESOURCES

Selected Bibliography

Baker, Peter, and Michael D. Shear. "Donald Trump Is Sworn In as President, Capping His Swift Ascent." *New York Times*, 20 Jan. 2017, nytimes.com. Accessed 26 Aug. 2020.

Blair, Gwenda. *The Trumps: Three Generations That Built an Empire*. Simon, 2000.

"Donald J. Trump Republican Nomination Acceptance Speech." *Donald J. Trump*, 21 July 2016, donaldjtrump.com. Accessed 8 Nov. 2016.

Further Readings

Allen, John. *The Trump Presidency*. ReferencePoint, 2020.

Edwards, Sue Bradford. *The Impeachment of Donald Trump*. Abdo, 2021.

Streissguth, Tom. *The 2016 Presidential Election*. Abdo, 2018.

Online Resources

To learn more about Donald Trump, please visit **abdobooklinks.com** or scan this QR code. These links are routinely monitored and updated to provide the most current information available.

Places to Visit

Republican National Committee
310 First St. SE
Washington, DC 20003
202-863-8500
gop.com
The official website of the Republican Party has information on the party.

Trump Tower New York
725 Fifth Ave.
New York, NY 10022
trumptowerny.com
Learn about the history of Trump Tower in New York City.

The White House
1600 Pennsylvania Ave. NW
Washington, DC 20500
202-456-1111
whitehouse.gov
Visit the official website of the White House or the White House itself to learn more about the history of the presidency.

SOURCE NOTES

Chapter 1. A New Kind of President

1. David Choi. "Nancy Pelosi Broke Tradition When Introducing Trump at the State of the Union, Leaving Out the Words 'Honor' and 'Privilege.'" *Business Insider*, 4 Feb. 2020, businessinsider.com. Accessed 28 Sept. 2020.

2. Sanya Mansoor. "Read the Full Transcript of President Trump's 2020 State of the Union Address." *Time*, 4. Feb. 2020, time.com. Accessed 28 Sept. 2020.

3. Mansoor, "Read the Full Transcript."

4. "Here's Donald Trump's Presidential Announcement Speech." *Time*, 16 June 2015, time.com. Accessed 28 Sept. 2020.

5. "Here's Donald Trump's Presidential Announcement Speech."

6. "Beyond Distrust: How Americans View Their Government." *Pew Research Center*, 23 Nov. 2015, pewresearch.org. Accessed 28 Sept. 2020.

7. "Trump Nation." *USA Today*, 2016, usatoday.com. Accessed 28 Sept. 2020.

8. Domenico Montanaro. "Trump's Base Is Shrinking As Whites without a College Degree Continue to Decline." *NPR News*, 3 Sept. 2020, npr.org. Accessed 7 Oct. 2020.

Chapter 2. Growing Up Trump

1. Gwenda Blair. *The Trumps: Three Generations That Built an Empire.* Simon, 2000. 225.

2. Michael D'Antonio. "The Men Who Gave Trump His Brutal Worldview." *Politico*, 29 Mar. 2016, politico.com. Accessed 7 Oct. 2020.

3. Blair, *The Trumps*, 225.

4. Donald J. Trump. *The Art of the Deal.* Random House, 1987. 78.

5. Trump, *The Art of the Deal*, 78.

6. Amy J. Rutenberg. "What Trump's Draft Deferments Reveal." *Atlantic*, 2 Jan. 2019, theatlantic.com. Accessed 7 Oct. 2020.

7. "Trump Says He's 'Made a Lot of Sacrifices,' in Response to Khizr Khan's Blistering DNC Speech." *CNBC*, 31 July 2016, cnbc.com. Accessed 7 Oct. 2020.

Chapter 3. Building New York

1. David. W. Dunlap. "1973: Meet Donald Trump." *New York Times*, 30 July 2015, nytimes.com. Accessed 7 Oct. 2020.

2. Tracie Rozhon. "Fred C. Trump, Postwar Master Builder of Housing for Middle Class, Dies at 93." *New York Times*, 26 June 1999, nytimes.com. Accessed 7 Oct. 2020.

3. Dunlap, "Meet Donald Trump."

4. "The Grand Hyatt Hotel." *The Trump Organization*, 2016, trump.com. Accessed 7 Oct. 2020.

5. "Donald J. Trump Biography." *The Trump Organization*, 2016, trump.com. Accessed 7 Oct. 2020.

6. Gwenda Blair. *The Trumps: Three Generations That Built an Empire.* Simon, 2000. 314–315.

7. Callum Borchers. "Donald Trump Hasn't Changed One Bit Since His First Media Feud in 1980." *Washington Post*, 18 Mar. 2016, washingtonpost.com. Accessed 7 Oct. 2020.

8. David Freedlander. "A 1980s New York City Battle Explains Donald Trump's Candidacy." *Bloomberg Politics*, 29 Sept. 2015, bloomberg.com. Accessed 7 Oct. 2020.

9. Charles V. Bagli. "Trump Paid Over $1 Million in Labor Settlement, Documents Reveal." *New York Times*, 27 Nov. 2017, nytimes.com. Accessed 7 Oct. 2020.

10. Blair, *The Trumps*, 325.

Chapter 4. Gambling on the Future

1. Gwenda Blair. *The Trumps: Three Generations That Built an Empire*. Simon, 2000. 338–340.

2. Charles V Bagli. "Trump Group Selling West Side Parcel for $1.8 Billion." *New York Times*, 1 June 2005, nytimes.com. Accessed 7 Oct. 2020.

3. Blair, *The Trumps*, 365.

4. David Segal. "What Donald Trump's Plaza Deal Reveals about His White House Bid." *New York Times*, 16 Jan. 2016, nytimes.com. Accessed 7 Oct. 2020.

5. Blair, *The Trumps*, 390–391.

6. Blair, *The Trumps*, 390–391.

7. Mark Singer. "Trump Solo." *New Yorker*, 19 May 1997, newyorker.com. Accessed 7 Oct. 2020.

8. Jane Mayer. "Donald Trump's Ghostwriter Tells All." *New Yorker*, 25 July 2016, newyorker.com. Accessed 7 Oct. 2020.

9. Blair, *The Trumps*, 381.

10. Monica Langley. "Trump's Adult Children Flex Muscle Inside Campaign." *Wall Street Journal*, 22 June 2016, wsj.com. Accessed 7 Oct. 2020.

Chapter 5. Building the Brand

1. David A. Graham. "The Many Scandals of Donald Trump: A Cheat Sheet." *Atlantic*, 23 Jan. 2017, theatlantic.com. Accessed 18 Nov. 2020.

2. Karen Yi. "Trump Lambasted by Casino Regulators." *Asbury Park Press*, 5 July 2016, app.com. Accessed 7 Oct. 2020.

3. Graham, "The Many Scandals of Donald Trump."

4. Graham, "The Many Scandals of Donald Trump."

5. Graham, "The Many Scandals of Donald Trump."

6. "40 Wall Street: The Trump Building." *40 Wall Street*, n.d., 40wallstreet.com. Accessed 7 Oct. 2020.

7. Steve Cuozzo. "Donald Trump Could Sell 40 Wall St. to Fund His Campaign." *New York Post*, 23 May 2016, nypost.com. Accessed 7 Oct. 2020.

8. Donald J. Trump with Kate Bohner. "Trump: *The Art of the Comeback* (Excerpt)." *New York Times Books*, 1997, nytimes.com. Accessed 7 Oct. 2020.

9. Charles V. Bagli. "Trump Sells Hyatt Share to Pritzkers." *New York Times*, 8 Oct. 1996, nytimes.com. Accessed 7 Oct. 2020.

10. Tracie Rozhon. "Fred C. Trump, Postwar Master Builder of Housing for Middle Class, Dies at 93." *New York Times*, 26 June 1999, nytimes.com. Accessed 7 Oct. 2020.

Chapter 6. Branching Out

1. "The Political Fray: The 1992 Run for the Presidency." *All Politics: CNN & Time*, 1996, cnn.com. Accessed 7 Oct. 2020.

SOURCE NOTES CONTINUED

2. Marc Fisher. "Donald Trump, Remade by Reality TV." *Washington Post*, 27 Jan. 2016, washingtonpost.com. Accessed 7 Oct. 2020.

3. Amy Bingham. "Donald Trump's Companies Filed for Bankruptcy 4 Times." *ABC News*, 21 Apr. 2011, abcnews.go.com. Accessed 7 Oct. 2020.

4. Bingham, "Donald Trump's Companies."

5. Bingham, "Donald Trump's Companies."

6. John Cassidy. "Trump University: It's Worse Than You Think." *New Yorker*, 2 June 2016, newyorker.com. Accessed 7 Oct. 2020.

7. Cassidy, "Trump University."

8. Scott Clement and Philip Rucker. "In New Poll, Support for Trump Has Plunged, Giving Clinton a Double-Digit Lead." *Washington Post*, 26 June 2016, washingtonpost.com. Accessed 7 Oct. 2020.

9. Shannon Travis. "Was He Ever Serious? How Trump Strung the Country Along, Again." *CNN*, 17 May 2011, cnn.com. Accessed 7 Oct. 2020.

10. Travis, "Was He Ever Serious?"

Chapter 7. Make America Great Again

1. "Here's Donald Trump's Presidential Announcement Speech." *Time*, 16 June 2015, time.com. Accessed 28 Sept. 2020.

2. Dylan Byers. "Donald Trump Has Earned $2 Billion in Free Media Coverage, Study Shows." *CNN*, 15 Mar. 2016, cnn.com. Accessed 28 Sept. 2020.

3. Jack Shafer. "Donald Trump's Phony War on the Press." *Politico*, 6 June 2016, politico.com. Accessed 28 Sept. 2020.

4. Donald J. Trump with Tony Schwartz. *The Art of the Deal*. Random House, 1987. 56.

5. Jose A. Del Real. "Trump, Pivoting to the General Election, Hones 'America First' Foreign Policy Vision." *Washington Post*, 27 Apr. 2016, washingtonpost.com. Accessed 28 Sept. 2020.

6. Michael D. Shear and David E. Sanger. "Chris Christie Made a Case against Hillary Clinton. We Fact-Checked." *New York Times*, 20 July 2016, nytimes.com. Accessed 28 Sept. 2020.

7. David Johnson and Chris Wilson. "Which Republicans Have Stopped Supporting Donald Trump?" *Time*, 13 Oct. 2016, time.com. Accessed 28 Sept. 2020.

8. Sarah Begley. "Hillary Clinton Leads by 2.8 Million in Final Popular Vote Count." *Time*, 20 Dec. 2016, time.com. Accessed 28 Sept. 2020.

Chapter 8. President Trump

1. Peter Baker and Michael D. Shear. "Donald Trump Is Sworn In as President, Capping His Swift Ascent." *New York Times*, 20 Jan. 2017, nytimes.com. Accessed 28 Sept. 2020.

2. "'Leave No Vacancy Behind': Mitch McConnell Remains Laser-Focused on Judges amid Coronavirus." *Vox*, 4 May 2020, vox.com. Accessed 13 Nov. 2020.

3. "Trump Hails 'Dawn of New Middle East' with UAE-Bahrain-Israel Deals." *BBC*, 15 Sept. 2020, bbc.com. Accessed 7 Oct. 2020.

4. Sanya Mansoor. "Read the Full Transcript of President Trump's 2020 State of the Union Address." *Time*, 4 Feb. 2020, time.com. Accessed 28 Sept. 2020.

5. Mary Papenfuss. "Trump Hails New Farm Aid Billions as Report Reveals Money Helps Wealthy, Southerners." *HuffPost*, 18 Nov. 2019, huffpost.com. Accessed 28 Sept. 2020.

6. Libby Nelson and Sarah Frostenson. "A Brief Guide to the 17 Women Trump Has Allegedly Assaulted, Groped, or Harassed." *Vox*, 20 Oct. 2020, vox.com. Accessed 13 Nov. 2020.

7. "Report of the Select Committee on Intelligence, United States Senate, on Russian Active Measures Campaigns and Interference in the 2016 US Election." *Senate Committee on Intelligence*, 2020, intelligence.senate.gov. Accessed 8 Oct. 2020.

8. Dana Milbank. "Trump Is Right. This Is a Witch Hunt!" *Washington Post*, 18 Mar. 2019, washingtonpost.com. Accessed 28 Sept. 2020.

9. Geoffrey Lou Guray and Patty Gorena Morales. "Mueller's Russia Probe, By the Numbers." *PBS NewsHour*, 22 Mar. 2019, pbs.org/newshour. Accessed 28 Sept. 2020.

10. Camila Domonoske and Richard Gonzales. "What We Know: Family Separation and 'Zero Tolerance' at the Border." *NPR*, 19 June 2018, npr.org. Accessed 29 Sept. 2020.

11. Jill Colvin, Liza Mascaro, and Zeke Miller. "Trump Signs Bill to Reopen Government, Ending Longest Shutdown in US History." *Chicago Tribune*, 25 Jan. 2019, chicagotribune.com. Accessed 29 Sept. 2020.

Chapter 9. A Tumultuous Final Year

1. "Trump Says Impeachment Inquiry Is a 'Hoax' Being Used for Political Gain." *Reuters*, 3 Dec. 2019, reuters.com. Accessed 29 Sept. 2020.

2. Stephen Collinson. "Trump Seeks a 'Miracle' as Virus Fears Mount." *CNN*, 28 Feb. 2020, cnn.com. Accessed 29 Sept. 2020.

3. Christina Morales, Allyson Waller, and Marie Fazio. "A Timeline of Trump's Symptoms and Treatments." *New York Times*, 6 Oct. 2020, nytimes.com. Accessed 8 Oct. 2020.

4. "The Twitter Presidency." *New York Times*, 2019, nytimes.com. Accessed 29 Sept. 2020.

5. Nolan D. McCaskill. "Trump Calls NYT Report on Tax Avoidance 'Totally Fake News.'" *Politico*, 27 Sept. 2020, politico.com. Accessed 12 Oct. 2020.

6. Morgan Chalfant and Brett Samuels. "Trump Prematurely Declares Victory, Says He'll Go to Supreme Court." *The Hill*, 4 Nov. 2020, thehill.com. Accessed 13 Nov. 2020.

INDEX

Access Hollywood, 65
Apprentice, The, 52, 54
Art of the Comeback, The, 46, 47
Art of the Deal, The, 21, 38–39, 61

bankruptcy, 44–45, 48, 49, 53–54
Barrett, Amy Coney, 73
Biden, Joe, 64, 83–84, 91–94
"birtherism," 56–57
border wall, 9, 56, 60, 69, 80, 81
Boston Globe, 40

casinos, 33–34, 44–45, 53
Celebrity Apprentice, The, 54
children
  Barron, 55
  Donald Jr., 28, 38, 40
  Eric, 37, 38, 40
  Ivanka, 37, 38, 40
  Tiffany, 48
Christie, Chris, 62
Clinton, Bill, 65
Clinton, Hillary, 62, 64–67, 79
Cohn, Roy, 25
Comey, James, 79
COVID-19, 86–90, 91, 92–93, 95
Cruz, Ted, 60
Curiel, Gonzalo, 56

debates, 61, 64–66, 92–93
Democratic National Committee, 79
deregulation, 70

election of 2016, 9, 11, 66–67
election of 2020, 93–95

Fair Housing Act of 1968, 25
Fordham University, 19

Garland, Merrick, 72
Gorsuch, Neil, 72
government shutdown, 81

hotels, 26–28, 34, 36, 43, 45, 48, 54, 78

immigration, 9, 59–61, 69, 80–81
impeachment, 6, 83–86, 95
inauguration, 69
Iran Nuclear Agreement, 75
Islamic State in Iraq and Syria (ISIS), 73–74

Kavanaugh, Brett, 72
Kew-Forest School, 16–17
Kim Jong-un, 74
Knauss, Melania, 49, 54–55

lawsuits, 25–26, 31, 48, 55, 56, 94–95
LiButti, Robert, 45

Maples, Marla, 48
Mar-a-Lago, 35, 36, 43, 54
McConnell, Mitch, 71
Mueller, Robert, 79–80
Mueller Report, 80

New York Military Academy (NYMA), 17–19
New York Times, 20, 25, 40, 92
North Atlantic Treaty Organization (NATO), 62–63

Obama, Barack, 56–57, 59, 62, 64, 72, 74

Paris Climate Agreement, 70
Pelosi, Nancy, 5–6
Pence, Mike, 63

real estate, 14, 17, 20–21, 23, 26, 33, 35–36, 38, 40, 43, 44, 52–53, 55
Reform Party, 51
Rosenstein, Rod, 79

Scalia, Antonin, 72
Schwartz, Tony, 39
Sessions, Jeff, 81
sexual abuse, 65, 72, 79
siblings
  Elizabeth, 13
  Fred Jr., 13, 36
  Maryanne, 13
  Robert, 13
Soleimani, Qasem, 75
State of the Union, 5–7, 77, 85
Stone, Roger, 51
supporters, 9–11, 60, 61
Swifton Village, 18–19, 21, 23

Taliban, 74
tariffs, 77–78
Trans-Pacific Partnership (TPP), 62
travel ban, 9, 70
Trump, Fred, 13–19, 20, 21, 24, 26, 44, 49
Trump Management Corporation, 23, 24, 25–26
Trump Tower, 30–31, 36, 39, 43, 59
Trump University, 55, 56
Twitter, 61, 89–90

US Constitution, 56, 84
US Department of Justice, 25
US House of Representatives, 5–6, 84–85
US Senate, 6, 71–73, 85
US Supreme Court, 71–73

Vietnam War, 20

Washington Post, 40
Wharton School of Business, 19–21
Whistleblower Protection Act, 84
Winklmayr, Ivana, 28, 34, 37–38, 48
World Health Organization (WHO), 87

Xi Jinping, 78

Zelensky, Volodymyr, 83

ABOUT THE AUTHOR

James Stuart

James Stuart is a freelance writer from central Minnesota who enjoys writing about and participating in the political process.

ABOUT THE CONSULTANT

Rachel Blum, PhD

Rachel Blum, PhD, is a political science professor at the University of Oklahoma in the Department of Political Science and the Carl Albert Congressional Research and Studies Center. Her research focuses on political parties in the United States, and she is the author of *How the Tea Party Captured the GOP: Insurgent Factions in American Politics*. She completed her PhD in government at Georgetown University in 2016.